C A N A D I A N
BATTLEFIELDS

———————{ *of the* }———————

FIRST WORLD WAR: A VISITOR'S GUIDE

REVISED SECOND EDITION

Terry Copp, Mark Humphries
Nick Lachance, Caitlin McWilliams, & Matt Symes

© LCMSDS Press of Wilfrid Laurier University Press

2 3 4 5 6 7 8 9 10
Printed and bound in Canada

Library and Archives Canada Cataloguing in Publication

Copp, Terry, 1938-
[Canadian battlefields 1915-1918]
   Canadian battlefields of the First World War : a visitor's guide / Terry
Copp, Mark Humphries, Nick Lachance, Caitlin McWilliams, & Matt Symes. -- Revised second edition.

Revision of: Canadian battlefields 1915-1918 : a visitor's guide / Terry Copp,
   Matt Symes, Nick Lachance. -- Waterloo, Ont. : LCMSDS, ©2011.
Includes bibliographical references.
ISBN 978-1-926804-16-3 (paperback)

1. World War, 1914-1918--Battlefields--France--Guidebooks. 2. World War, 1914-1918--Battlefields--Belgium--Guidebooks. 3. World War, 1914-1918--Campaigns--Western Front. 4. Canada. Canadian Army--History--World War, 1914-1918. I. Symes, Matt, author II. Lachance, Nick, 1982-, author III. Humphries, Mark Osborne, 1981-, author IV. McWilliams, Caitlin, 1987-, author V. Title: Canadian battlefields of the first world war: a visitor's guide.

D528.C67 2015   940.4'144   C2015-902558-3

ISBN 978-1-926804-11-8

Book Design: Caitlin McWilliams
Distributed by: Wilfrid Laurier University Press / University of Toronto Press

LAURIER CENTRE
for MILITARY
STRATEGIC and
DISARMAMENT
STUDIES
WILFRID LAURIER UNIVERSITY

Laurier Centre for Military Strategic and Disarmament Studies
Wilfrid Laurier University
Waterloo, Ontario
N2L 3C5 Canada
www.canadianmilitaryhistory.ca

CONTENTS

By 1917, soldiers of the British Expeditionary Force, of which the Canadians were a part, sent home eight million letters per week. [CWM 19920085-344]

PREFACE TO THE SECOND EDITION
MARK HUMPHRIES

THIS NEW AND COMPLETELY revised second edition of our visitor's guide to the Canadian battlefields on the Western Front 1915-1918 adds to our series of guidebooks, published by the Laurier Centre for Military Strategic and Disarmament Studies (LCMSDS), to the Canadian battlefields in Europe. Our first titles, originally published in 1994-1995 for the 50th anniversaries of the Normandy invasion and the end of the war, have also gone through several editions and revisions which eliminated chapters on the First World War in favour of an in-depth treatment of the 1944-1945 campaign in Northwest Europe. We now present a user-friendly guide to the Canadian experience on the Great War battlefields in Belgium and France.

This book is not intended to be an exhaustive review of battles or battlefields. We have selected events and tour itineraries on the basis of fifteen years of experience leading student groups overseas and have highlighted the most important books and websites to encourage further readings. But we feel that most visitors will find that the guidebook provides enough information to allow for a basic understanding of what happened and why it happened that way.

New in this edition are five walking the battlefields sections which allow visitors to walk over the ground of some of the most important actions fought by Canadian troops during the Great War. We chose these walks (as opposed to many others) because they are relatively easy to do without a professional guide on-site, are short in duration, and they take the visitor across terrain that is not much modified from 1914-1918. We suggest that readers who plan to do these walks in advance read the relevant chapters in Tim Cook's excellent books *At the Sharp End* and *Shock Troops*. They might also bring copies with them. G.W.L. Nicholson's official history is available both online and in a new edition published by McGill-Queen's University Press.

In this edition, Mark Humphries and Terry Copp rewrote the history and are responsible for errors, omissions, and interpretive judgements. Their students and colleagues at Wilfrid Laurier University, Mount Royal University, and l'Université de Montréal and especially those who have participated in the "Cleghorn Battlefield Tours" have provided the opportunity to test out ideas and advance our understanding of the war experience. Our annual trips to the battlefields of France and Belgium are supported by generous donations from John and Pattie Cleghorn, Brad and Sara Dunkley, and Neville 'Monty' Monteith as well as funding from the Department of History, the Faculty of Arts, and Office of the Vice-President Academic at Wilfrid Laurier University. In this respect, we owe a special thanks to David Monod, Mike Carroll, Deborah MacLatchy, and Max Blouw as they not only support our overseas field schools, but also provide space and funding for LCMSDS. This second edition of the guidebook was also specially funded by a donation from John Cleghorn. It would not have been possible without his generosity and vision.

Mark Humphries and Terry Copp re-wrote the tour section from the first edition text that was written by Prof. Copp, Matt Symes and Nick Lachance. Matt Symes had overall responsibility for the design of the first edition. Caitlin McWilliams re-designed this second edition. Nick Lachance again worked with Google Earth images to create the battle and tour maps while Mike Bechthold developed the overview maps for the first edition which are used again here. Most of the modern day photos were taken by Nick Lachance, Caitlin McWilliams, or Matt Symes on either the 2009 or 2010 Cleghorn Study Tours, or the 2013 War and Memory Tour. Eric McGeer and Brandey Barton were gracious enough to edit various versions of the guide. Eric's guidance with the appendices, suggestions for war art, as well as the modern day photos he contributed have added immensely to the final product. For their work on the first edition, we must thank Caleb Burney, Jordan Burrows, Elise De Garie, Geoff Keelan, Mike Lakusiak, and Brendan O'Driscoll.

Our thanks also to Joe Anderson, Matt Baker, Mike Bechthold, Carl Bouchard, Trevor Ford, Michel Fortmann, Geoff Hayes, Andrew Iarocci, Geoff Keelan, Kellen Kurschinski, David Monod, Lianne C. Leddy, Lyndsay Rosenthal, and Ben Toews.

Our long-standing partnership with the Canadian War Museum (CWM), and especially Susan Ross and Laura Brandon, has allowed us to incorporate some of the outstanding war art from the First World War which has greatly enhanced the final product. Where you see CWM in the caption, this refers to the Beaverbrook Collection of War Art held at the Canadian War Museum. Every effort has been made to give proper reference to the illustrations we have used. We are grateful to Google for permission to use their copyright imagery to illustrate the battlefields.

We would be happy to answer questions about battlefield touring. Contact Mark Humphries at mhumphries@wlu.ca or Terry Copp at tcopp@wlu.ca. Please direct general inquiries to admin@canadianmilitaryhistory.ca

48th Highlanders, 12th Infantry, & 10th Royal leave Toronto for camp, with the Toronto Armouries in the background.

CANADA AT WAR

MOST OF THE WORLD REMEMBERS the First World War as a time when "innocent young men, their heads full of high abstractions like Honour, Glory and England… were slaughtered in stupid battles planned by stupid Generals." English-speaking Canadians, while generally accepting this view, have supplemented it with an imaginative version of a war in which their soldiers won great victories and forged new national identities. Both of these approaches have served to promote literary, political and cultural agendas of such power that empirical studies of what actually happened during the war have had little impact upon the prevailing memory of the war and its significance. Recently, a new generation of scholars have challenged approaches driven by romantic stories about nation-building and heroic sacrifice, insisting that "the reality of the war and the society which produced it" are also worthy of study. If historians are to continue to study the past to further understand what actually happened, and why it happened that way, they need to remember that the men and women who participated in events like the First World War were not concerned with the views of later generations. The meaning of their war was constantly changing and they tried to act in ways that were consistent with their own values.

It is clear, for example, that while Canadians were surprised that the assassination of an Austrian archduke should lead to war, those citizens interested in world affairs had long been aware of the possibility of such a conflict. The enmity between Germany and France, the alliance system, and the increasingly bitter rivalry of the German and British Empires had been topics of informed discussion throughout most of the decade that preceded the war. The "naval question" along with reciprocity or free trade with the United States, dominated pre-war political debate and sensitized many of those normally indifferent to such topics. Canadians were divided on issues of war and peace and especially divided on military and naval expenditure precisely because they thought they understood what was at stake.

French Canadian opinion, at least within Quebec, was almost universally opposed to any form of military expenditure that might underwrite automatic Canadian participation in foreign wars. Within English-speaking Canada there were sharp divisions between Imperialists, Canadian Nationalists, anti-militarists and declared pacifists. While newspapers like the *Montreal Star* and the *Toronto Mail and Empire* offered strong support for military preparedness, the *Toronto Globe*, the *Methodist Guardian* and the voice of the western farmer, *The Grain Growers Guide*, were equally adamant about the dangers of militarism. David Mackenzie has edited a collection of essays by prominent Canadian scholars, *Canada and the First World War*, which touches on these and other key issues.

Canada's leaders played no part in the decision for war in 1914 and it is literally true that Canada went to war because Britain had decided to go to war. This statement, while accurate, does little to help us make sense of the events of August 1914 in Europe or in Canada. To understand we must answer three different questions: (1) Who was believed to be responsible for the outbreak of war? (2) Why was Britain involved? (3) What kind of war was it going to be? The answers to these questions seemed obvious to those English speaking Canadians who read the newspapers and participated in the Dominion's political life. Germany was threatening the peace of Europe and violating Belgian neutrality as part of an attack on France. Britain was defending France against German aggression and coming to the assistance of Belgium. The war was likely to be over by Christmas after decisive battles between standing armies, but it might last until 1915. The answers would have been less clear-cut to the hundreds of thousands of immigrants from Central and Eastern Europe who came to Canada in the two decades preceding 1914, to pacifists and those opposed to militarism, and to Aboriginal Canadians who had

A Toronto street car, headed "to Berlin," is used to recruit for the No. 1 Construction Battalion. [CWM 19940081-004]

a complicated relationship to the Crown. Even so, many members of these groups at least temporarily put aside their differences and supported the war effort either because they shared or had internalized mainstream beliefs or because they felt that the war provided an opportunity to gain social or political status.

The young Dominion had experienced a surge of growth between 1896 and 1913, nearly doubling its population from 5 to 8 million. This growth was mainly sustained by increased immigration which had come from all over Europe (including from Germany and Austria, Canada's future enemies) but mainly from Britain and the United States. Most English speaking Canadians, including new Canadians, saw themselves first and foremost as British subjects which made sense. Canada was a small nation compared to the United States and there was a whole school of intellectual and creative thought dedicated to ensuring that Canada found its path to greatness by seeking a greater role within the British Empire. Non-English speaking Canadians, which included most of Quebec and the large pockets of German immigrants at Berlin, Ontario and Ukrainians on the prairies, probably thought little about these imperial-nationalist dreams—so long as they did not prove disruptive to their own lives. Most also had few lingering loyalties to the old countries. Although defining a mainstream view is difficult before opinion polling, in general we can say that the urban, English-speaking, middle-classes believed that Canada was part of an important Empire and must actively support the mother country in a just war which Britain had tried to prevent. Of course, from a historical perspective this view of the origins of the war is too simplistic and ignores Britain's own imperial ambitions and colonial legacies, but today the scholarly consensus is that Germany was indeed waging an aggressive war although questions of morality are less clear-cut. Two of the most interesting essay collections on the origins of the war are Keith Wilson's *Decisions for War 1914*, and Holger Afflerbach and David Stevenson's *An Improbable War*. Margaret MacMillan's *The War that Ended Peace* is the most readable narrative.

The country's commitment to the war effort was never in doubt but Canada could not provide any immediate assistance to Britain. Wilfrid Laurier's attempt to create a Canadian Navy, able to defend Canada's coasts and assist in the protection of imperial sea lanes, ended with his defeat at the polls in 1911. The Liberal-controlled Senate then blocked Prime Minister Robert Borden's Naval Aid Bill which offered direct financial assistance to the Royal Navy. As a result, in 1914 the Royal Canadian Navy possessed only two obsolescent light cruisers, *HMCS Rainbow*, and *HMCS Niobe*.

Canada's regular army was comprised of only 3,000 officers and men as well as some 70,000 volunteers serving in the militia. Under the energetic if eccentric leadership of Sam Hughes, Minister of Militia since 1911, fifty-six new armouries and drill halls were built and training camps created or expanded. Hughes is usually remembered for his misguided commitment to the Ross Rifle, a Canadian-designed and manufactured hunting weapon which proved deficient under combat conditions. But if Hughes is to be condemned for his errors of judgment, he must also be remembered for encouraging more realistic training, marksmanship, the acquisition of modern guns for the artillery, and the expansion of the militia. The raising of 30,000 men for the First Canadian Contingent in the late summer of 1914 must surely be regarded as a significant accomplishment no matter the Minister's other faults. Ronald Haycock's biography *Sam Hughes*, published in 1986, is still the basic source for Hughes' career, but Tim Cook's 2010 book *The Madman and the Butcher* provides a well-written account of Hughes as well as his conflict with Corps Commander Arthur Currie.

Whatever view one takes of Hughes, it is evident that no Canadian field force could possibly have gone into action on a European battlefield in 1914. This did not stop the Minister from trying. On 6 August he sent 226 night telegrams directly to unit commanders of the militia ordering them to interview prospective recruits and wire lists of volunteers for overseas service to Ottawa. Hughes bypassed existing mobilization plans and had the Canadian Expeditionary Force (CEF) assemble at a new, yet to be built, embarkation camp at Valcartier near Quebec City.

One legacy of Hughes' decision to scrap the mobilization scheme was the failure to designate a French-Canadian battalion in what was to become the First Canadian Division. French-speaking recruits were shunted to the 14th Battalion

Sir Sam Hughes (centre, with binoculars) and a party of officers on the Somme, August 1916. [CWM 19920044-575]

The 1st Canadian Infantry Battalion at Valcartier. [CWM 19740416-003]

(Royal Montreal Regiment) where they formed one of the four companies in a unit where English was the dominant language. The Maritime Provinces were also excluded from representation in the new numbered battalions of the CEF. Given the apparent support for the war that was evident in Quebec in 1914 when even Henri Bourassa, the *nationaliste* icon, briefly supported Canadian participation, the absence of a French-Canadian battalion until the 22nd (the "Van Doos") went into action in September 1915 was bound to effect recruiting in Quebec and New Brunswick.

Who were the men who volunteered to go to war in 1914? Desmond Morton suggests that "for the most part, the crowds of men who jammed into the armouries were neither militia nor Canadian-born." Most, he argues, were recent British immigrants anxious to return to their homeland in a time of crisis, especially when Canada was deep in a recession which had created large-scale unemployment. The best available statistics suggest that two thirds of the First Contingent "were British born and bred." Command of the First Division went to a British officer, Lieutenant-General Sir Edwin Alderson, but Hughes appointed Canadians to command the brigades, battalions, and artillery regiments. Morton's book *When Your Number's Up* is highly recommended.

Newfoundlanders were still mourning the loss of more than 300 sealers hunting on the ice flows in a spring blizzard when news of war reached the colony. The response was nevertheless enthusiastic and in the absence of a recent British immigrant population, recruits were drawn from a cross section of town and outport communities. Less than a quarter million people lived in Newfoundland in 1914 but thousands volunteered to serve in the Newfoundland Regiment, which served as a separate entity and was never part of the CEF, and the Royal Navy.

Imperial ties were no doubt basic to this response but many were drawn to serve by the promise of decent pay and chance to see the world.

The men who gathered at Valcartier were supposed to be at least 5'3" tall with a chest measurement of 33.5 inches, between 18 and 45 years of age, and ready to serve for one year "or until the war ended if longer than that." Officers received from $6.50 a day for a Lieutenant-Colonel to $3.60 for a Lieutenant. Non-commissioned officers could earn as much as $2.30 a day while the basic rate for a soldier was $1.10. The Canadian Patriotic Fund soon provided additional support for families from private donations. The Fund, with chapters across Canada, offered support only after investigating the recipients and then provided assistance on a sliding scale which paralleled the army's rates of pay. Desmond Morton's *Fight or Pay* tells the story of the Patriotic Fund. A dollar a day was not far below the income of a junior clerk or unskilled labourer and far above the cash paid to a farm worker. The army was thus an attractive proposition to many single men seeking escape from the dull routines of work or the harsh experience of unemployment. A large number of married men also volunteered but Sam Hughes, who insisted participation had to

A photographer captured the physical differences amongst those who formed the Canadian Expeditionary Force. [CWM 19920044-284]

be voluntary in every sense of the word, decided that "no recruit would be accepted against the written protest of his wife or mother." Newspapers reported that "long lists of men were struck off the rolls" because of this regulation.

As the Canadian Expeditionary Force and the Newfoundland Regiment departed for England, a Second Contingent, which would become the Second Canadian Division, was authorized. This decision on 7 October was made in the context of the dramatic retreat of the British Expeditionary Force from Mons, the German advance on Paris, and the so-called "miracle" at the Battle of the Marne which was said to have saved France from immediate defeat. If the war was seen as a romantic adventure in early August, by October the harsh reality of high casualties — although as yet no Canadians — and the prospect of a German victory now fostered a more realistic view. By October, Canadian newspapers had also devoted significant column-space to describing the plight of the Belgian people fleeing the German invasion which supported the view that Canada was fighting a moral war against an evil enemy. Voluntary organizations including farm groups, churches and *ad hoc* committees responded with offers of money, food, clothing, and plans to aid Belgian orphans and refugees. Meanwhile, Sir Wilfrid Laurier and other prominent French Canadians travelled to Ottawa to persuade Prime Minister Robert Borden to authorize recruiting for a French language unit.

With Hughes away in England, Borden agreed and the result was the 22nd Battalion or Van Doos. Recruiting French Canadians to an army steeped in British Imperial traditions and English-only training manuals meant that officers would have to be fully bilingual with French limited to internal use. The 22nd joined the 25th (Nova Scotia) and the 26th (New Brunswick) battalions and together with the 24th (Victoria Rifles, Montreal) formed the 5th Canadian Infantry Brigade. These units helped to increase the ratio of Canadian to British-born recruits, but still less than forty percent of the Second Division was born in Canada.

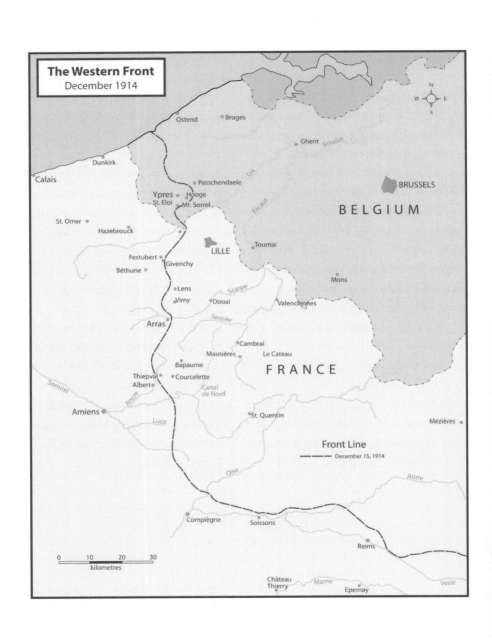

The Western Front
December 1914

Ostend
Bruges
Ghent
Scheldt
Dunkirk
Calais
BRUSSELS
Passchendaele
Ypres
Hooge
St. Eloi
Mt. Sorrel
Lys
Escaut
BELGIUM
St. Omer
Hazebrouck
LILLE
Tournai
Festubert
Givenchy
Béthune
Mons
Lens
Scarpe
Vimy
Douai
Valenciennes
Arras
Sensée
Cambrai
Masnières
Le Cateau
Bapaume
FRANCE
Thiepval
Courcelette
Albert
Somme
Canal
de Nord
Ancre
Amiens
Luce
St. Quentin
Mézières

Front Line
December 15, 1914

Oise
Aisne

0 10 20 30
kilometres

Compiègne
Soissons
Reims
Château
Thierry
Marne
Epernay
Vesle

ENGLAND AND FRANCE 1915

THE FIRST CONTINGENT ARRIVED in Britain on 14 October and reached their tented camp on Salisbury Plain near Stonehenge just in time for the worst, wettest winter in recent memory. Over the next four months they trained to join the British Army in Flanders as a standard infantry division of 18,000 men. The establishment included three brigades each of 130 officers, 4,000 men and 272 horses. Each of these consisted of four infantry battalions of approximately 900 men each, commanded by a lieutenant-colonel. A battalion, in turn, was made up of four rifle companies, each divided into four platoons. Additional firepower was provided by two sections of two Colt machine guns per battalion. Three divisional artillery brigades, equipped with modern 18-pounder field guns and a 60-pounder Heavy Battery, provided additional firepower.

There is no consensus among historians as to how well-prepared the Canadians were when they entered the line in February 1915. Desmond Morton describes the Canadians as "woefully unready." John Swettenham, the author of *To Seize the Victory*, still a very useful survey of the Canadian military effort, emphasized the problems of the Ross Rifle and other difficulties with equipment. Bill Rawling's

Edgar Bundy, "Landing of the First Canadian Division at Saint-Nazaire." [CWM 1971061-0110]

important study, *Surviving Trench Warfare: Technology and the Canadian Corps 1914-1918*, reminds us that "the Canadian artillery was not able to fire its guns until the end of January 1915 and then was allotted just 50 rounds per battery." "The gunners," he writes, "would have to wait until the move to France to gain any real experience with the tools of their trade." Rawling concludes that the First Division was "hardly a well-trained formation," but notes that trench warfare was new to the "professional armies of Europe as well." The official Canadian history of the war, G.W.L. Nicholson's *Canadian Expeditionary Force, 1914-19*, quotes the commander of the British Expeditionary Force, Field Marshal Sir John French, who reported that the Canadians were "well trained and quite able to take their places in the line." This is the sort of thing generals are required to say and has little other value.

Andrew Iarocci's important study of the training and initial battle experience of First Canadian Division, *Shoestring Soldiers*, presents a detailed analysis of the preparatory period. He argues convincingly that "the Canadians who landed in France in February 1915 were well prepared for battle by contemporary standards." Once in northern France, they were paired with veteran British battalions, rotated through the trenches and exposed to repeated exercises in rapid fire, fire control and close combat drill. As he writes, "Every infantry soldier in the division had an opportunity to visit the front lines and work with a British 'buddy' before regrouping into his own platoon for a stint in the trenches." While this experience was undoubtedly valuable, it is also important to keep in mind that it was still not a regular division and more experienced British officers were sceptical. Most brigade commanders and senior battalion officers had never been in combat nor had a regular military posting; only a few like Brigadier General Richard Turner had served in the Boer War. The divisional artillery was also attached to British units and officers went forward to observe the guns in action and to give Canadian FOOs (Forward Observation Officers) "many helpful hints." The importance of camouflaging gun positions was stressed and courses on technical matters were pursued. What the Canadians lacked in experience they made up for in confidence. Captain H.D.G. "Harry" Crerar expressed a common opinion when he wrote, "I'm sure the Canadian Division will do as well as the rest of them for they have the right spirit ... and their training by this time is pretty well completed to the standard of Imperial troops."

In early March 1915, First Canadian Division went into the line for the first time on its own, taking over 6,400 yards of trenches near Armentières close to the Franco-Belgian border. Their first task was to improve the trench defences, a job for the divisional engineering field companies. The First Brigade Canadian Field Artillery located its batteries of 18-pounders near Fleurbaix while the First Canadian Heavy Battery set up positions further back. The front line was at the foot of the Aubers Ridge, a position which provided the Germans with an overview of the Allied lines.

The Canadians and two British divisions were part of IV Corps, First British Army. The Corps commander, Lieutenant-General Henry S. Rawlinson, was responsible for planning an attack on Neuve Chapelle, the first British offensive of the war. While the 7th and 8th British Divisions and the Indian Army Corps advanced on the village, the Canadian Division to the left was to "maintain its position" and "open artillery, rifle and Maxim gun fire on their immediate front and Fromelles village in order to hold the enemy to his ground and prevent reinforcements being sent to Aubers." Rawlinson was reasonably confident that his Corps could capture Neuve Chapelle which was in a small salient on the low ground, but he believed that General Douglas Haig, the Army Commander, was too optimistic about their chances of securing the ridge beyond. In the event, Neuve Chapelle was taken but no further advance onto the ridge proved possible although for a brief moment the German front had in fact been breached. As the German official history noted, "the intermediate position was unprotected and hanging out in the open." However, the tired troops who made the advance lacked the energy or artillery support to push forward into the gap and it was sealed the next day by German reserves brought in from elsewhere along the front. This modest achievement was hailed as a victory despite 13,000 British and Indian casualties. The Canadians had played a supporting role, suffering about a hundred casualties from enemy shelling. The initial and unexploited breakthrough cast a long shadow over British decision-making for the next eighteen-months—if only the reserves and cavalry had been closer to the front and more artillery available a real advance seemed tantalizingly possible. Neuve Chapelle, though, was a dangerous mirage.

A convoy of six different motor vehicles passes in review at Rockcliffe, Ottawa. A variety of vehicles equipped the First Canadian Contingent. [CWM 19910109-152]

Second Battle of Ypres - 22-24 April 1915

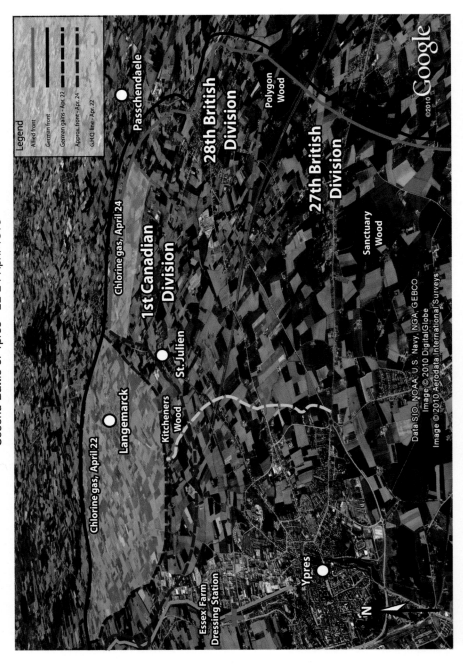

FLANDERS FIELDS 1915-1916

EARLIER IN THE WINTER, General Joseph Joffre asked Field Marshal Sir John French to take over parts of the Ypres Salient held by the French Army. This, Joffre argued, would allow his armies to mount a new offensive with adequate reserves. In late March, three divisions, including First Canadian, were transferred to Second British Army with the Canadians joining V British Corps in the center of the salient, adjacent to French troops. V Corps was commanded by Herbert Plumer who later became known as one of the most cautious and meticulous generals serving on the Western Front. But in April 1915, British generals were firmly committed to offensive action believing that spring would bring a new campaigning season, restoring mobility to the Western Front. So as the Canadians prepared to take over positions at the apex of the salient, Plumer's first communication was ordered Alderson and his subordinate commanders to make "definite plans" as to where an offensive action "should be carried out."

One important consequence of the belief that trench-lock was a temporary problem was that French and British troops paid little attention to the state of their lines as they expected to soon vacate them. The trenches which the Canadians took over from the French were nothing like the neat, well maintained earthworks they had read about in the manuals. A "Report on the Condition of the Trenches"

Cyril Barraud, "First Glimpse of Ypres." [CWM 19710261-0021]

prepared by Captain T. C. Irving of the Canadian Engineers noted that, "we found on our arrival conditions to be extremely bad." One section some 1,650 yards long "consisted of 15 isolated portions of trench… The water level is about two feet down below the surface of the ground with numerous shell holes and also a section of the trench behind partially filled with water… In front of these sections are numerous bodies in a decomposed state lying on the surface of the ground…." Most trenches had breastworks made of "heaps of mud" that provided little protection. It was not uncommon for digging to uncover hastily buried bodies from the earlier battles for Ypres. Canadian engineers worked to improve the defences and drain parts of the line. In contrast, the German Army had been preparing more or less permanent defensive systems since the previous November.

British and Canadian officers were sharply critical of the condition of the trenches left by the French army, but the problems were partly product of the very different doctrine the French had adopted. By 1915 the French army had learned to rely on its quick firing 75mm guns and infantry reserves positioned to counterattack when a German advance began. An early version of defense-in-depth, the forward trenches were lightly held and, given conditions on the salient, little was done to strengthen these outposts.

British doctrine was very different. The front line was to be fully occupied and held to the last man. The corps and divisional commanders had emphasized this policy and rejected the option of planning for a phased withdrawal to much stronger second line defenses. The French had begun to build such a position two to three miles behind the front known to the British as the GHQ Line. This still incomplete position was protected by a continuous belt of barbed wire, six yards wide and redoubts sited to provide good fields of fire.

After Neuve Chapelle and a French Army attack in Champagne, which General Joffre insisted was a success because the Germans had to use troops "drawn from other parts of the line" to stop it, both the French and British armies planned to launch new offensives in late April or early May. The Germans, who had been forced to transfer troops to the east to assist the Austro-Hungarian armies, decided to mount an attack to disguise their weakness in the west and to demonstrate their continuing capacity to take the initiative. The German view of Second Ypres is outlined in *Germany's Western Front, Volume II: 1915*, a translation of the German official history edited by Mark Humphries and John Maker.

Attempting to collapse the Ypres Salient by an attack from the north was an obvious possibility. As an added bonus, the direction of attack provided a good opportunity to try out a new weapon: chlorine gas. The German Army's experiment with chlorine gas as a method of breaking the stalemate on the Western Front has been re-examined by Tim Cook in his book *No Place to Run*. The Canadians were, he reminds us, sent into a salient which "protruded into the Germans lines like a rounded tumour, eight miles wide and six miles deep." The positions they took over from the French covered 4,500 yards north of Gravenstafel Ridge and were overlooked by German observers on Passchendaele Ridge to the east.

Eight days after their tour of duty began, a period of quiet settled over the salient broken by an intense artillery barrage beginning in the late afternoon. As Cook writes, "along with the shells came an ominous grey-green cloud four miles long and half a mile deep." The gas crept upon the 45th Algerian and 87th French Divisions. He continues:

> One by one the French guns fell silent only to be replaced by screaming choking Algerians running into and past the Canadian lines…The victims of the gas attack writhed on the ground. Their bodies turned a strange gas-green as they struggled to suck oxygen into their corrupted lungs. The chlorine attacked the bronchial tubes, which caused the membranes to swell into a spongy mass and ever-increasing amounts of fluid to enter from the bloodstream. The swiftly congested lungs failed to take in oxygen, and the victims suffocated as they drowned in their own fluids.

The 13th Battalion, Montreal's Black Watch, together with Algerian troops who were on the edge of the gas cloud formed a new defensive line along the Ypres-Poelcappelle Road. A composite force held St. Julien and with the arrival of the 7th British Columbia battalion at what would become known as "Vancouver Corner," a further German advance from the north would meet organized resistance. Unfortunately, senior commanders including Lieutenant-General Alderson responded to a request from a French liaison officer to mount a counterattack in support of a proposed advance by the Algerian division.

Member of the Canadian Army Veterinary Corps and a horse wearing gas masks. [CWM 19930003-453]

The extensive bandages on these wounded Canadian soldiers
may indicate that they have suffered the effects of flame or
mustard gas. [CWM 19920085-540]

Given the collapse of that formation, we now know that such an advance was unlikely, but the idea of immediate counterattacks to regain lost ground was deeply imbedded in military doctrine and Alderson, without checking on the state of the Algerians, ordered two Canadian battalions, the 10th and 16th, to retake "Kitchener's Wood." That night, the battalions charged the clump of trees routing the enemy, but as there was no Algerian advance they were forced to withdraw suffering heavy casualties.

Early the next morning a second counterattack in support of the French Army was launched by the 1st and 4th battalions. Once again the Canadians were left on their own, clinging to the lower slope of Mauser Ridge. The two Canadian battalions suffered 855 casualties, 50 percent of their rifle strength. More than 600 of these were wounded and heroic efforts were needed to evacuate them from the battlefield.

Both Canadian battalions established their Regimental Aid Posts (RAP) at a farmhouse east of the canal. The walking wounded and those on stretchers were brought to the RAP for first aid but the area was under German artillery fire. At 10 a.m., two medical officers from 1st Field Ambulance, with wagons and 100 men, braved the shellfire, crossing the canal on a pontoon bridge to set up a Collecting Post (CP) at the farmhouse. After basic triage the seriously wounded were stabilized, loaded on the horse-drawn wagons and taken across the canal to safety.

As the battle raged and hundreds of additional wounded men arrived, the farmhouse suffered direct hits, including tear gas shells. Captain E.L. Stone moved the CP to the west side of the canal, working his teams forward from this more secure position. Colonel J.G. Adami, whose book, *The War Story of the C.A.M.C. (Canadian Medical Corps) 1914-1915*, offers a narrative of the medical corps at Second Ypres, described Stone's efforts. "By dusk the wounded ceased to come in and now he heard of a large farm half a mile beyond… he found it full of wounded, with no medical officer… Capt. Stone made this farm his next Collecting Post." He and his men "were too busy to do any dressings. There was no time to take notes and make records. They were fully occupied in looking after the creature comforts of the wounded, tagging them and sending them on."

Early on the morning of 24 April, as the Canadians and the first British reinforcements struggled to build new defensive positions, a second gas attack began. The 15th and 8th Battalions of Canada's Second Brigade, holding the original lines in what was now the apex of the salient, saw the gas drifting towards them and urged each other to "piss on your handkerchiefs and tie them over your faces." As legend has it, chemistry students in the army recalled that urine contained ammonia which might neutralize the chlorine. Cook quotes Major Harold Matthews' vivid memories of the moment:

It is impossible for me to give a real idea of the terror and horror spread among us by the filthy loathsome pestilence. It was not, I think, the fear of death or anything supernatural, but the great dread that we could not stand the fearful suffocation sufficiently to be each in our proper places and to be able to resist to the uttermost the attack which we felt must follow and so hang on at all costs to the trench we had been ordered to hold.

Courage and determination were, however, no proof against the full force of the gas and as the Canadians slowly retreated, wounded and severely gassed soldiers were abandoned to become prisoners. A new defensive line some 1,000 metres further back was established with the assistance of British troops and the next day the Germans launched a series of conventional attacks near the village of St. Julien where the famous "Brooding Soldier" Canadian War Memorial now stands. After the German advance south of the village was halted, General Alderson was ordered to recapture St. Julien and "re-establish our trench line as far north as possible." This order compounded the growing chaos and led to more heavy losses. Stopping the Germans was one thing, retaking ground in a salient which was valued for reasons of Belgian pride and British prestige quite another. On 26 April yet another attack into the German positions was launched. The Lahore Division of the British Indian Army advanced until gas, used for the first time defensively, broke the impetus of the attack.

The Canadians emerged from the battle with horrendous casualties, over 6,000 men including 1,410 who became prisoners of war. This casualty rate, 37 percent of the troops engaged, would never be exceeded, not even at the Somme. The British and Canadian press lauded the Dominion's achievement and the enemy acknowledged their "tenacious determination," but behind the scenes there were serious conflicts over the conduct of the battle including sharp criticism of Brigadiers Arthur Currie and Richard Turner both of whom made questionable decisions at key moments of the battle. Many Canadian officers were equally unhappy with the performance of senior British officers.

News of the gas attack and the valour of the country's soldiers reached Canada on 24 April before the battle was over. The newspapers reported that Canadian "gallantry and determination" had saved the situation but hinted at heavy losses. The Toronto *News* described the mood:

> Sunday was one of the most anxious days ever experienced in Toronto, and the arrival of the officer's casualty list only served to increase the feeling that a long list including all ranks was inevitable. Crowds scanned the newspaper bulletin boards from the time of arrival of the first lists shortly before noon, until midnight, while hundreds sought information by telephone.

Historian Ian Miller, in his book *Our Glory and Our Grief*, describes the dawning awareness that whole battalions had been devastated. At first it was impossible to believe that battalions such as the 15th, made up of men from Toronto's 48th Highlanders, had been wiped out and the press assumed that many were prisoners of war. When full lists were available in early May, the truth was apparent: "half the infantry at the front have been put out of action." As Jonathan Vance argues in *Death So Noble*, the events of the spring of 1915 transformed the war from a great adventure to a great crusade. A week after the gas attack, the *Lusitania* was torpedoed off the coast of Ireland with the loss of 1,369 civilians including 150 children. Newspapers across Canada published heart-rending stories about the victims and survivors of the sinking alongside further accounts of the fighting in the Ypres Salient.

Canadians were horrified by these acts which most believed violated international law, underscoring the belief that British war effort was a moral necessity. This was particularly true after the first gas attack when, to cite just one example, a letter from the front printed in the Toronto *World* informed readers that:

> … the dead are piled in heaps and groans of the wounded and dying never leave me. Every night we have to clear the roads of dead in order to get our wagons through. On our way back to base we pick up loads of wounded soldiers and bring them back to the dressing stations.

The censors could do little to prevent the publication of such letters and they proved equally unable to control the content of articles on the war. One attempt to stop the publication of Robert W. Service's gritty descriptions of his experiences as an ambulance driver was ignored by editors determined to print front line reports from the popular author and poet. Service's description of the "Red Harvest" of the trenches with its images of "poor hopeless cripples" and a man who seemed to be "just one big wound" left no room for doubt about the ugliness of war.

F.H. Varley's "Gas Chamber at Seaford" depicts a training exercise in Seaford, England. [CWM 19710261-0772]

This photograph of the ruined battlefield near Festubert was taken in the spring of 1919. [CWM 19920044-938]

FESTUBERT AND GIVENCHY

THE REVERSE SUFFERED BY Second British Army at Ypres did not lead to any change in plans to support a new French offensive intended to secure the Lorette Spur north of Arras and the Vimy Ridge beyond to the west. The British contribution was to be a new attack on Aubers Ridge meant to draw reserves away from the Vimy sector. The French attack began on 9 May and made good progress despite heavy casualties although the British attack failed in every respect. The French even reached the crest of Hill 145 ("The Pimple") atop Vimy Ridge although they were later pushed back. Despite enormous losses, it had been the largest single advance since the end of the mobile war the previous summer. For a brief moment, the German line seemed to have been breached and the attack only petered out the men became exhausted and outstripped their artillery. Like Neuve Chapelle, this convinced Joffre and French that the only thing preventing bigger gains had been the limited availability of artillery shells and a lack of immediate infantry reserves. As a result, Joffre decided to continue the battle and again the British were called to support the attack with another diversionary attack, this time further south at Festubert. Here Haig's First Army planned to make a pincer movement preceded by a lengthy bombardment rather than the "Hurricane," a forty minute barrage, used unsuccessfully at Aubers Ridge. For the first time, a prepared attack was to begin at night. The cost of this more "successful" action, which gained modest but meaningless ground and did little to improve French fortunes, was between 12,000 and 16,000 casualties.

The Canadians, who had lost one third of the 18,000 men in the division at Ypres, had been partially reinforced from the reserve battalions brought to England with the First Contingent. Despite the best efforts of officers and NCOs, two weeks was not enough time to integrate these soldiers into existing rifle companies. One may reasonably ask: why was Third Canadian Brigade, which had borne the brunt of the battle in the salient, placed under command of 7th British Division and pressed into battle on 18 May? The answer is not altogether satisfying but it illustrates two important points. First, the Canadians were never an autonomous fighting force on the Western Front, even if some people like Sir Sam Hughes thought they should be; they were always just one part of a much larger British Expeditionary Force subject to British strategy and decision-making. Second, even though there was no unified command structure to unite the French and British armies, Sir John French (and later Douglas Haig) frequently had to make unpalatable decisions in the interests of strategic coordination. The French army was, after all, many times larger than the British army and so long as that was the case, the offensive burden had to fall on Joffre's troops with the British playing a supporting role which effectively subordinated British commanders to French. At the same time, both Joffre and French had to consider the needs of their Russian and (after April) Italian allies as well as the political requirement that he remain on the offensive lest neutral nations like Romania, Bulgaria, or Greece side with the Central Powers. In the spring of 1915, Sir John had little choice but to support the renewed French offensive at Vimy and with Second Army still licking its wounds and the First reeling from the attack on 9 May, the Canadians seemed as ready a body of troops as any.

Sent over the top within hours of relieving British units, the 14th and 16th Battalions made scant progress before digging in. The rest of the division arrived the next day and, despite Alderson's plea for time to study the situation before committing his troops, Haig insisted on immediate action. Two days of intense close combat for what would be called the Canadian Orchard ensued. The price: 2,468 casualties.

Coming so soon after the struggle in the salient, Festubert was a shock to many Canadians. Brigadier Arthur Currie complained bitterly about the lack of

These French and English posters were meant to encourage recruitment by highlighting the Canadians' heroic stand at the battles of St. Julien (Ypres) and Festubert. [CWM 19750046-010 & CWM 19880207-002]

preparation and inadequate support while Sam Hughes wrote a scathing attack on Alderson which he sent to Prime Minister Borden and Lord Kitchener. As always, Hughes went off the deep end but his criticisms should not be entirely ignored. The fruitless attacks at Festubert which Hughes described as "attempting to gain a few yards... with no preconceived plan of an effective drive to smash the enemy" are an accurate picture of the engagements that cost First British Army a further 16,000 casualties. Yet in typical fashion, Hughes also ignored the bigger strategic picture. Had the Canadians not been sent to do the job, another British brigade would have gone in their place. Given that the war had become a moral struggle, negotiating peace was no longer a viable political option and so France, supported by the British Expeditionary Force (BEF), continued to press the offensive. What now appear to us as costly, pointless offensives, seemed to the commanders of 1915 to be bringing the Entente one step closer to victory.

As historians Robin Prior and Trevor Wilson argue in *Command on the Western Front*, for French and Haig, the tactical lesson of Festubert was that a new attempt to break through the German defences and exploit into open country might succeed if a longer preliminary bombardment was employed and the attack made along a wider frontage. When the British were again called on to support renewed French attacks north of Arras, the battle for Givenchy began with 211 guns firing for 48 hours before two British divisions attacked in the early evening of 15 June. Givenchy quickly turned into another costly disaster for British troops. The First Canadian Brigade under Brigadier Malcolm Mercer played a supporting role, protecting 7th British Division's flank. Neither the British division nor the Canadian Brigade made any significant progress and the operation was called off on 18 June. The response of both Rawlinson, the corps commander, and Haig was typical: both blamed a lack of drive amongst the infantry for the failure to make headway. Yet as Prior and Wilson point out, Rawlinson drew an important lesson from the battle with serious implications for future operations. "I much doubt," he is quoted as saying in a report written soon after the battle, "if any kind of artillery fire however accurate and well sustained will have the desired effect unless it is sufficient to bury the garrisons in the deep dug-outs they have now constructed, and this is a matter of chance."

Overall, Allied losses in May and June totalled more than 200,000 men, appalling figures that for beg the question why these offensives were not called off—especially in light of observations like Rawlinson's. But during the war, each action seemed to bring with it the promise of victory or at least a tantalizing glimpse of the break through that seemed always to be just out of reach. It was also impossible to ask the generals to stop ordering offensives so long as the political will to fight remained strong. Even when they did not feel confident of victory, as Rawlinson did not before Givenchy, there seemed little choice but to press on. Britain had obligations to France and both had to support their Russian and Italian allies. It was also risky to cede the initiative to Germany and Austria-Hungary who were still vying for the affections of the neutral nations. So in the summer of 1915, British and French commanders convinced themselves that with more men and more and better shells for the artillery including ones filled with gas, they could break the German defences—judgments which seemed to flow logically from their experiences at Neuve Chapelle and Aubers Ridge. Lord Kitchener, the British War Minister, who was striving to create a 'New Army' which would place fifty divisions in the field, was less sure. He was preparing for a long war but admitted that he too had no idea how it might be won. It is evident that the British generals, like their French and German counterparts, did not know how to get men across interlocking zones of machine gun, mortar and artillery fire to close with the enemy. They were equally unable to exploit any breach in their opponents' defensive position if it should happen to occur.

Some historians have accused senior British officers, with a few outstanding exceptions, of demonstrating a profound lack of imagination and initiative in the early years of the war. To a certain degree this is undoubtedly true. The first suggestions for a tracked armoured vehicle which could overcome barbed wire and cross trenches were made in Britain during the fall of 1914 but initially the army was not interested. Instead experiments were carried out by a "landships committee" formed by Winston Churchill, through his control of naval expenditures. But it is also true that when the first such vehicles, known for security reasons as "tanks," were demonstrated in the fall of 1915 the army was quick to order them into production for use the next summer, though another full year passed before large numbers were available. Steel helmets, which saved many lives, were issued by the French in early 1915 but British and Canadian troops, like the Germans, waited another year before helmets became standard issue. The Germans also made early use of trench mortars but it took eleven months to authorize the mass production of the British-invented Stokes mortar, although this was largely due to ammunition manufacturing problems rather than a lack of support from the officer corps. The public was not aware of these problems, but they were told of the shortage of Allied machine guns and shells which was said to account for German success in trench warfare. New technologies took time to be develop, prove, and then integrate onto the battlefield and it was impossible to predict which innovations would bear fruit and which would prove to be dead-ends.

Even the most important new technologies required both military and political champions to ensure that they would be produced in large enough quantities to have an effect on the battlefield. For example, the machine gun movement, which became a popular crusade in Britain, was launched in Canada by John C. Eaton of the department store family who donated $100,000 to purchase armoured cars equipped with Colt machine guns. The concept of motorized armoured machine gun carriers was an initiative of Raymond Brutinel, a former French officer and immigrant to Canada, who organized "the first motorized armoured unit formed by any country during the war." Brutinel's First Canadian Motor Machine Gun Brigade was reinforced by the batteries created in Canada and championed by the Borden government, though the static conditions on the Western Front provided little opportunity for mobile warfare. Before 1918 the brigade was used primarily in a fire support role.

During the second half of 1915 and the early months of 1916, no Canadian formation was committed to a major battle. The Second Division, raised in the fall of 1914, arrived in France in September 1915 and went through an extensive training process including time in the trenches. Major-General Sam Steele, an authentic western Canadian hero, commanded the division during training but Sir John French and Lord Kitchener insisted on an experienced commander offering "any British officer on the unemployed list" for the job. Sam Hughes and Prime Minister Robert Borden, determined to see Canadians in command posts, approved a compromise. A Canadian Corps under Alderson was established and

Brutinel's Motor Machine Gun Brigade.

two Canadian Brigadiers, Richard Turner and Arthur Currie, became divisional commanders. The older Steele was to take charge of Canadian troops in England.

After the series of costly and frustrating battles in the first half of 1915, the British High Command understood enough of the mechanics of trench warfare that it hoped to postpone participation in a major offensive until more high explosive shells and Kitchener's new armies were available. Far ranging and converging successes by the Central Powers on the Eastern Front, in Serbia, Italy and at Gallipoli made a new fall offensive in the West a strategic necessity and French demands for British assistance in yet another attempt to capture Vimy Ridge forced Sir John French to agree to a battle in the flat terrain punctuated by slag heaps immediately north of Lens.

In planning what became the Battle of Loos, Sir John and Douglas Haig aimed to punch a hole in the German line and drive on towards Douai and Valenciennes. Acknowledging the lessons of the previous spring, French positioned his reserves close to the front while Haig was forced to use chlorine gas to compensate for the still inadequate supplies of artillery ammunition. Again the battle was mostly a disaster. Along some parts of the front, the wind suddenly changed direction and blew the gas back on the attacking troops while British artillery failed to cut the German wire in most places. In the centre, though, the British infantry managed to capture Loos through massive wave attacks and, as happened the previous March, suddenly found themselves looking out into an undefended gap in the German

The destroyed Cloth Hall at Ypres was an iconic symbol of the war. The city was bombarded by the Germans but never captured. After the war, Belgians rebuilt the Cloth Hall as it had once stood. [CWM 19710261-0334]

lines. There British divisions had advanced in a variety of formations rather than simple long lines of infantry under the protection of a primitive creeping barrage that neutralized enemy defenders rather than attempting the impossible task of destroying their defences. Although French husbanded a significant reserve of infantry and cavalry under his personal control, he delayed releasing them until after it was allegedly too late to exploit the gap. With hindsight we can say that it probably would have made little difference. In the end, some 50,000 British soldiers, almost half of whom were killed or missing, were lost at Loos which led to the dismissal of Sir John French later that December. Haig would be promoted to command the BEF in his place, escaping much of the blame for a poorly planned offensive thanks to French's poor handling of the reserves. The lessons of Loos only served to confirm British tactical thinking: more artillery would be needed to break the German line while masses of infantry arrayed in depth would be needed to capture the objectives; any exploitation would have to be made quickly before the Germans could react which seemed to suggest that the cavalry might still play an important role. Readers interested in Haig's own writings should consult Gary Sheffield and John Bourne's *Douglas Haig: War Diaries and Letters*. J.P. Harris has written the most balanced account of Haig's role in the war in *Douglas Haig and the First World War*.

The Canadians spent the summer and fall of 1915 holding the line in the Ypres salient with Plumer's Second Army. It was a miserable period of trench warfare punctuated with raids and small company level attacks but no major actions. The Canadians were out of the line in December when the Germans conducted an experiment with a new gas. The attack at Messines began with the release of chlorine and an intense shrapnel bombardment. The enemy then fired artillery shells containing phosgene hoping to create panic among the defenders whose gas masks could not cope with high concentrations of the new gas. Despite heavy casualties, including 120 who died from inhaling phosgene, the British troops held.

During the last weeks of 1915, both adversaries developed plans for operations in 1916. At the Chantilly Conference held on 6 December 1915 a vague agreement to launch coordinated offensives on the Russian, Italian and Western fronts was reached with spring 1916 as the preferred date. The German commander Von Falkenhayn pre-empted these plans with his decision to wage an attritional battle at Verdun beginning in February. The allies great offensive in the West would become the Somme campaign. The best overview of the role of the French Army at Verdun and elsewhere is Robert Doughty's *Pyrrhic Victory*. Paul Jankowski's *Verdun: The Longest Battle of the Great War* offers a detailed account.

St. Eloi Craters - 2-16 April 1916

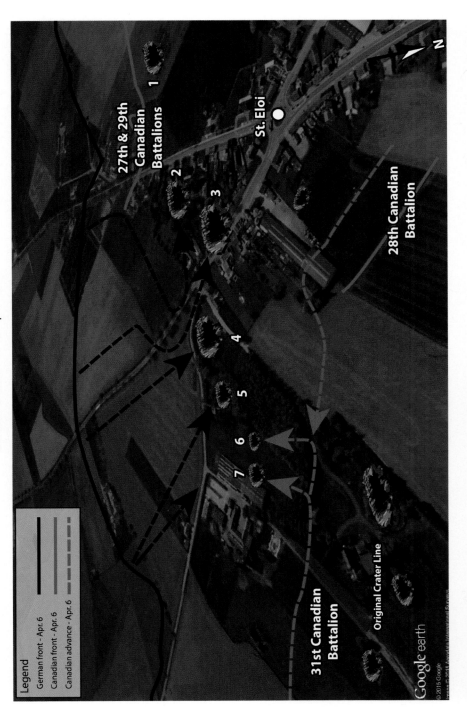

Legend

German front - Apr. 6
Canadian front - Apr. 6
Canadian advance - Apr. 6

27th & 29th
Canadian
Battalions

28th Canadian
Battalion

31st Canadian
Battalion

Original Crater Line

St. Eloi

1
2
3
4
5
6
7

N

Google earth

© 2015 Google
Image © 2015 Aerodata International Surveys

ST. ELOI CRATERS 1916

FALKENHAYN ORDERED A SERIES of small-scale diversionary attacks on other fronts and on 14 February German forces in the Ypres sector began an assault which captured a key position known as the "Bluff." Haig, newly in command of the BEF, already disliked General Plumer, commanding the Second British Army, who decided to commit substantial forces to recover the lost position and to hit back at the enemy by capturing the feature known as the "Mound" nearby at St. Eloi, an excavated earth pile that overlooked the British positions. A British tunnelling company had completed work on six shafts that reached under the German trenches where large explosive mines had been prepared. The Third British Division was ordered to attack as soon as the mines under the enemy were exploded. The Mound was practically destroyed and the new craters added to the complexity of the ground in no-man's-land. And then the rains began.

The Canadian Corps was scheduled to relieve V British Corps after the new position was gained, but after heavy British losses and a confused series of

Aerial reconnaissance photo of the St. Eloi craters.

SUMMARY OF OPERATIONS,
2nd Canadian Division,
from April 1st to April 7th, 1916.
----

1.   My Division was relieved, during the period under review, in
the KEMMEL area by the 50th Division, and the 2nd Canadian Division
in turn relieved the 3rd Division. These changes began on March
31st and were completed on April 5th. The artillery of these
Divisions have not relieved each other as yet.
     The command of the former 3rd Division area passed to me at
3 p.m. on April 3rd.

2.   As soon as the 6th Canadian Infantry Brigade took over the trench
(from DIEPENDAALDEEK to the CANAL) work was vigorously started under
the direction of the C.R.E. improving the trenches and deepening an
reversing the captured German trenches south of the line of craters
in the vicinity of ST. ELOI.   In addition a support line immediate
south of the craters was sited and work started on this.

3.   The hostile bombardment was heavy from the time of our arrival
greatly interfered with continuous work in the trenches but good
progress was made. During the 5th instant, the left half of the
captured trenches were practically destroyed by 6" and 8" shell fir
On the night of April 5th/6th the 27th Canadian Battalion was relie
in the new front line trenches by the 29th Canadian Battalion. On
this night working parties numbering 1,000 were employed on the wor
of consolidating the new position. This relief and the return of
working parties was carried out without incident.
     At dawn on the morning of April 6th a very intense hostile
bombardment opened on all out trenches and works on the Divisional
front, causing great destruction to the defensive works and inflict
heavy casualties upon the garrisons.
     Our artillery immediately opened a heavy bombardment, and abou
the same time the enemy launched an infantry attack which reached
craters Nos. 2 and 3.
     During the day of April 6th all rearward works were manned by
the 4th Canadian Infantry Brigade, and bombing attacks were launche
against the lost craters.   The attack against crater No.2 by 27th
Canadian Battalion was unable to penetrate the hostile barrage. Th
attack against crater No.3 by 28th Canadian Battalion succeeded in
reaching craters 5 and 6 but were unable to proceed further. A
company of the 28th Battalion followed this bombing attack on the
early morning of April 7th and relieved the bombers.   They also ma
a start at digging in, in craters 4 and 5.   These crater garrisons
suffered heavy casualties and were relieved on the night of April
6th /7th where they are still holding on.
     In the early morning of April 7th, the 27th Canadian Battalio
was relieved by the 21st Canadian Battalion in the "P" trenches and
at 3.20 p.m. on the same day the 4th Canadian Infantry Brigade was
ordered to relieve the 6th Canadian Infantry Brigade

4.   The artillery of the Canadian Corps and 5th Corps co-operated
with the artillery of the Second Army during these operations.

5.   On the night of April 6th/7th four German prisoners were captu
Two of them were of the 216th Regiment, and one of the 214th R.Reg
     On the night of April 7th/8th, five prisoners were captured,
of the 215th Reserve Regiment and three of the 63rd Machine Gun
Company.

                              (Sgd) R.E.W.Turner, Major-Genera
8th April,1916.   Comdg.,2nd Canadian Divisi

engagements the troops were exhausted and the relief had to be conducted before the new line was fully consolidated. Despite protests from Major-General R.E.W. Turner, commander of the 2nd Canadian Division. who personally crawled through mud to survey the situation, the Canadian Corps was given the unfortunate task of carrying out a relief in the midst of an unfinished and still chaotic battle. While the Canadians were still settling into their lines, the Germans counterattacked after an hour-long bombardment capturing the large craters numbered 2, 3, 4, and 5. Over the next few days the Canadians became confused about the precise position of their line and ultimately had to accept that the new position was lost. The best account of the struggle in the "open grave" of St. Eloi is to be found in Tim Cook's book *At the Sharp End*. His chapters "The Murder Hole" and "Defeat and Scapegoats" offer a graphic description of life and death and the post-battle search for someone to blame for this ugly catastrophe and the 1,300 Canadian casualties. The document at right is an official report of operations written by Turner which covers the first week of fighting at St. Eloi.

The battle of St. Eloi led to another crisis in command relationships when Alderson, the Corps commander, sought to dismiss Turner and one of his brigadiers for alleged incompetence. The new British Commander-in-Chief, General Sir Douglas Haig, refused to confirm the decision because of "the danger of a serious feud between the Canadians and the British… and because in the circumstances of the battle for the craters mistakes are to be expected." Canadian historians have been divided on the issue, some siding with Alderson and others Turner. Whatever the verdict, only political interference from Hughes and his representative Sir Max Aitken (later Lord Beaverbrook) saved the Canadians, ultimately costing Alderson his job as Corps commander. In the final analysis, the case against Turner is difficult to wholly refute. It is easy to be sympathetic as the situation was impossibly confused and Turner could only do his best under very trying circumstances. But as Tim Cook argues, he was also in charge when his men made the mistake of assuming they were occupying one line when they were really on another several hundred yards away. Ultimately these poor performances at St. Eloi and Second Ypres would lead to Turner's "promotion" to command Canadian troops in England the following autumn.

The Canadians, now including the Third Division, spent the spring of 1916 in familiar positions in Flanders. The enemy was still able to shell the salient from several directions making life in the forward lines both miserable and very dangerous. Many Canadian (and British) officers expressed their bitter opposition to orders to hold and attempt to expand the Ypres Salient. Sam Hughes, always suspicious of decisions made by professional British soldiers, created a major controversy when he publicly denounced the policy.

Mount Sorrel - 2-14 June 1916

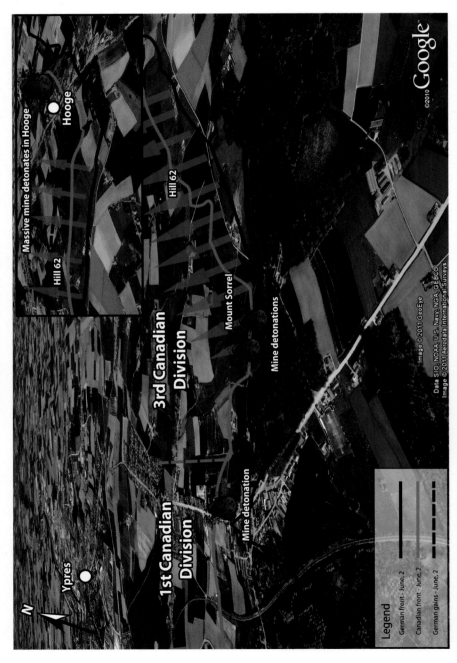

Massive mine detonates in Hooge

Hooge

Hill 62

Hill 62

N

Ypres

Mount Sorrel

1st Canadian Division

3rd Canadian Division

Mine detonations

Mine detonation

Legend

German front - June, 2

Canadian front - June, 2

German gains - June, 2

Data SIO, NOAA, U.S. Navy, NGA, GEBCO
Image © 2011 GeoEye
Image © 2011 Aerodata International Surveys

©2010 Google

MOUNT SORREL 1916

THE FALLOUT FROM ST. ELOI which cost Alderson and a British divisional commander their jobs had no impact on Plumer who had orchestrated the disaster. He continued to command Second Army. The new Canadian Corps commander was Sir Julian Byng, a veteran of the South African war who had commanded the Cavalry Corps in France before earning good reports for his leadership in supervising the withdrawal of colonial forces, including the Newfoundland Regiment, from Helles and Suvla Bay in Gallipoli. Byng was to acquire a considerable reputation as the Canadian Corps commander but in 1916 he had less than three months experience leading an infantry corps on a quiet sector of the front.

Byng was the grandson of a Field Marshal and a prominent member of the English aristocracy. Like many other British officers, he retained his schoolboy nickname, "Bungo." His self-confidence and easy manner won him friends throughout the army and especially within the Canadian Corps. Historians have repeatedly lavished praise on Byng. Tim Cook argues "he was the single most

Mary Riter Hamilton, "Sanctuary Wood." [LAC 1988-180-21]

Post-battle image of the June 1916 Mount Sorrel battlefield. The debris is all that remains of a dugout and shelter destroyed by artillery fire. [CWM 19920044-977]

important figure in transforming the Canadian Corps into a battle-hardened formation." Perhaps so, but in early June 1916 the problems confronting Canadian and British troops in the Ypres Salient could not be fixed by a Corps commander, however charismatic.

When Byng took over, the Canadians were responsible for the sector of the Ypres Salient from the Menin Road to south of St. Eloi. The recently formed Third Division commanded by Major-General Malcolm Mercer held the left of the line clinging to the only part of the Ypres ridge still in Allied hands, what the official historian, G.W.L. Nicholson, called "a flat knoll called Mount Sorrel and two slightly higher twin eminences, 'Hill 61' and 'Hill 62,' the latter known as Tor Top." From Tor Top a "broad span of largely farm land, aptly named Observatory Ridge, thrust nearly a thousand yards due west between Armagh Wood and Sanctuary Wood."

Despite the tactical importance of the ridge-top positions, Second Army failed to respond to growing signs that a German attack was imminent. The Canadians who took over the sector were just beginning to make changes when the attack struck. Two German divisions of the Wurttemburg Corps, employing the heaviest bombardment yet used in the area, overwhelmed the Canadian positions. Both General Mercer and Brigadier-General Williams, commander of the 8th Brigade, were killed early in the battle and this no doubt added to the confusion. The Germans, who had planned a three stage operation, quickly dug in overlooking Ypres.

Byng, who had been with the Corps less than a week, ordered an immediate counterattack that proved to be a costly failure. He then stepped back and organized an intensive artillery-based attack employing two composite brigades of First Division. The original line was restored following an equally heavy Canadian bombardment and quick advance on 13 June. The two weeks of close combat, including the loss of Hooge, a village on the Menin Road, cost the Corps close to 9,000 casualties including hundreds of shell shock cases.

The Canadian Memorial at Hill 62. [Nick Lachance]

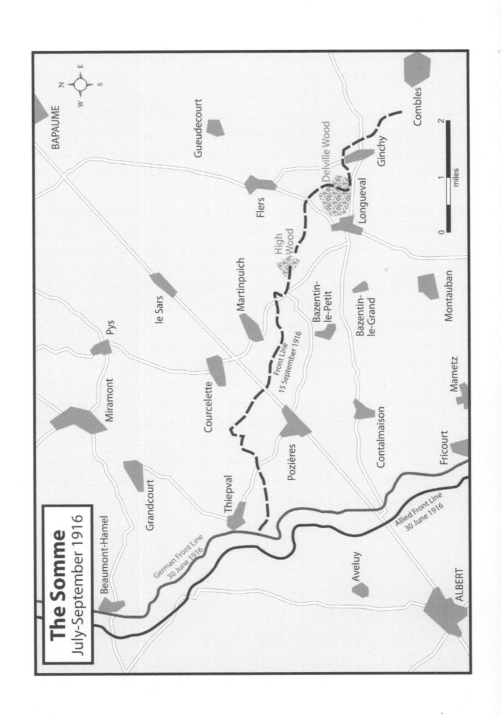

The Somme
July–September 1916

N · E · S · W

BAPAUME

Gueudecourt

Combles

Delville Wood

Ginchy

Flers

Longueval

High Wood

Martinpuich

Bazentin-le-Petit

Bazentin-le-Grand

Montauban

Pys

le Sars

Courcelette

Front Line
15 September 1916

Contalmaison

Mametz

Miramont

Pozières

Fricourt

Grandcourt

Thiepval

German Front Line
30 June 1916

Aveluy

Allied Front Line
30 June 1916

Beaumont-Hamel

ALBERT

0   1   2
miles

THE SOMME

WHILE THE CANADIANS ENDURED life and death in the Ypres Salient, German Chief of Staff Erich von Falkenhayn began the battle of Verdun. This offensive, he told the Kaiser, might win the war, especially if combined with unrestricted submarine war against all merchant shipping. Falkenhayn hoped to "bleed the French Army white" by seizing positions the French would be determined to counterattack at great cost. The battle — the longest of the war — that began on 21 February 1916, was still raging when Russia launched its most successful operation, the "Brusilov Offensive" on 4 June. The Germans, who had begun accumulating reserves to meet the projected Allied offensive in the Somme, were forced to transfer fifteen divisions to the east, ending any possibility of continuing offensive operations at Verdun.

The Somme offensive is now chiefly remembered for the disastrous first day, 1 July 1916 when 21,000 British soldiers were killed and 35,000 wounded, but the battle continued with pauses for re-organization for four and a half months. The political and military leaders of France and Britain had selected the Somme valley as the logical site for a major offensive because it was the only place where the

Aerial photograph of a gas attack on the Somme battlefield using metal canisters of liquid gas. [CWM 19700140-077]

Beaumont-Hamel - 1 July 1916

armies of the two nations could fight side-by-side. Unfortunately, there was nothing else to recommend an area of rolling chalk hills that the enemy had fortified during 1915. The Germans created their first line of defences on the forward slopes of ridge lines. Two belts of barbed wire protected three trenches: outpost line, main position and reserve, each approximately 160 metres apart. Where possible, fortified villages like Beaumont, Hamel and Thiepval were incorporated into the defences where deep dugouts served to protect troops. The German second line 3,000 metres to the rear was protected by yet more barbed wire and a series of small fortresses acting as strongpoints. A third position was under construction when the attack began.

Haig had entrusted planning for the Somme to Fourth Army's commander, Sir Henry Rawlinson, who initially envisioned a "bite and hold" approach in which the infantry would make a relatively short advance supported by heavy concentrations of artillery fire designed to destroy the enemy wire and defences. His initial plan for Fourth Army called for "seizing points of tactical importance which will provide us with good observation and which the Germans will counterattack." The object was "to kill as many Germans as possible with the least possible loss" but he also ignored the wisdom of his own experience. Although the fighting at Aubers Ridge and Givenchy had shown that artillery alone could not destroy well prepared German defences, Rawlinson's plan assumed that the artillery would do the lion's share of the work, allowing the infantry to walk across No-Man's-Land and occupy their old positions. Haig used Rawlinson's optimism about the power of artillery to argue that the limited plan was too cautious and asked Fourth Army's commander to arrange for an initial advance that would capture both the first and second German positions across a 25

Captain Kenneth Keith Forbes, "Canadian Artillery in Action." [CWM 19710261-0142]

Battle of Courcelette - 15 September 1916

Bapaume

Candy trench

Sugar factory

Courcelette

Sugar trench

15th British Division

2nd Canadian Division

3rd Canadian Division

Albert

Legend

German front line
Allied front line
German retreat
German trenches

N

Google
©2010
Image © 2011 IGN-France

kilometre front after a six day preliminary bombardment. Three cavalry divisions were available for exploitation. As Prior and Wilson argue in their book *The Somme*, both Rawlinson and Haig were to blame for the subsequent disaster: Rawlinson for his over-reliance on artillery and Haig for broadening the scope of the attack.

The results of both Rawlinson's and Haig's optimism may be viewed at a Canadian National Historic Site, the Beaumont-Hamel Newfoundland Battlefield and Memorial. Here the VIII British Corps with three divisions suffered enormous losses. There as elsewhere, the outcome of the battle had little to do with the tactics adopted and everything to do with the nature of the German defences and the success of the artillery preparation. As Prior and Wilson demonstrate, the leading brigades tried a variety of techniques all along the line from "blob" formations to line-based wave attacks to creeping barrages to cross No-Man's-Land. The problem was not the lack of experience of the officers and men; the catastrophe was rooted in the decision to ask too much of the available artillery and in the strength of the German defences.

The Germans first position included Y Ravine protected by the extensive barbed wire on the Hawthorn Ridge, a particularly formidable obstacle which British miners had tunnelled under and planted 18,000 kilograms of explosives. For reasons that have never been satisfactorily explained, the Corps commander, Lieutenant-General Sir Aylmer Hunter-Weston, an officer known for arrogance and the bullying of subordinates, decided to set off the explosives ten minutes before the attack began alerting the defenders waiting on the reverse slope. The 86th and 87th Brigades of 29th Division found much of the wire uncut and the German defences largely intact. The decision to commit the reserve, 88th Brigade including the Newfoundland Regiment, to a battle that was already lost has been blamed on

A dressing station on the Somme in 1916, with soldiers looking startled as a shell lands in the near distance.
[CWM 20020094-001]

The zig-zag lines on the left are communication trenches leading back towards the rear areas in this October 1916 photograph of the Somme. [CWM 19920085-125]

poor communication which led the division commander, Major-General de Lisle, to believe that one of his brigades was through the German forward defences. Both the Essex Regiment and the Newfoundlanders were subjected to intense machine gun and artillery fire and were unable to reach the German front line: "Dead men can advance no further."

The 29th Division lost 5,000 men, including 90 percent of the men of the Newfoundland Regiment (272 killed, 438 wounded), VIII Corps suffered 14,000 casualties or about half of its rifle strength. The Newfoundland Regiment and much of the rest of the division and Corps had to be rebuilt, returning to full strength at the Somme in October. A smaller version of the famous Caribou Memorial marks the Gueudecourt battlefield where the battalion captured a major German strongpoint.

The Canadian Corps was transferred to the Somme in August and began training for the specific circumstances of the terrain. By that time, the British Army's operations had bogged down and the Canadians were to take over the sector that bedevilled the Australian Corps at Pozières. The Australians had suffered more than 8,000 casualties in a failed attempt to take the well-fortified Mouquet Farm. Prior and Wilson note that total casualties for the period 7 August to 12 September in the sector "cannot have been much short of 20,000." The Canadians relieved the exhausted Australians in preparation for yet another attempt to break through the German defences.

This time Haig believed a mid-September offensive would yield better results because a new weapon, the tank, would be available to support the assault divisions. Once again Haig insisted on a breakthrough plan to seize all three German positions "with a view to opening the way for the cavalry." Writing in his diary, he recorded his belief in the imminent collapse of German morale and the necessity of making the attack "as strong and violent as possible, and plan to go as far as possible." By September, the British Commander-in-Chief had convinced himself that the Somme battle had not been fruitless, but was the first phase in an attritional struggle that would prepare the way for a complete German collapse. He expected that the collapse would begin with the 15 September push so he also issued orders for a general advance by the rest of the British Army to begin as soon as it started.

The Canadian Corps joined General Hubert Gough's Reserve Army. The First Division took over the entire Corps front while Second and Third Divisions rehearsed their parts in what was to become known as the Flers-Courcelette battle. The Canadians were just one of four Corps committed to action on 15 September. Eleven divisions therefore had to share just 56 tanks. The seven allocated to the Canadians could hardly have been expected to be a decisive factor.

The Second Canadian Division, which led the way, relied on a rolling barrage to take their objectives, assigning a mopping up role to the tanks. The "Sugar

Medical orderlies tend to the wounded in a trench during the Battle of Courcelette in mid-September 1916.
[CWM 19920044-639]

Factory" proved to be heavily fortified but fell to a well-rehearsed attack from three directions as the barrage lifted. Just two of the six tanks sent into action engaged the enemy. Mopping up occupied much of the morning and at 1800 hours the 5th Brigade, commanding Brigadier A.H. Macdonnell, renewed the advance with the 22nd and 25th Battalions taking Courcelette. The artillery again led the way but both battalions reported brief intense encounters. They then dealt with the inevitable counterattacks, seventeen of them over the next four days.

The division and its commander, Major-General Richard Turner, had been under a cloud since the battle of the St. Eloi Craters. Courcelette, a well-managed tactical victory changed the reputation of the division but did little to restore Turner's tarnished reputation. The casualty toll of 1,283 included a very high proportion (714) killed in action but in the surreal world of the Western Front this was a relatively low-cost victory. Unfortunately in the days that followed, casualties mounted as the Canadians were required to continue the struggle to secure the German position known as Regina Trench.

The battle for Courcelette may have been just another in a series of bloody, attritional encounters but the capture of the village was seen as a success for the 5th Brigade and especially the 22nd Battalion. The achievement of the corp's only French Canadian unit was headline news in both Quebec and the rest of the country. Courcelette became identified with the "Van Doos" and for a short period, until conscription was introduced in May 1917, French and English-speaking Canadians were united in their support of the men on the front line.

On 26 September, First Canadian Division attempted to reach Regina Trench as part of a four division assault on Thiepval Ridge. The capture of Thiepval village and Mouquet Farm by two British divisions and limited gains by the Fourth Army allowed claims of another victory but the costs were enormous and there was no sign of the expected German collapse. Continuing attacks in the Somme could no longer be justified by reference to Verdun and Haig now emphasized his belief that the enemy was near the breaking point. Rain storms that turned much of the battlefield into a muddy morass did not bring an end to repeated attacks, including the final assault on Regina Trench that was secured by the Fourth Canadian Division on 11 November 1916. For a detailed description of the Canadian experience, see Tim Cook's *At The Sharp End*.

The Somme cost the British 432,000 casualties—the fighting strength of twenty-five infantry divisions. French casualties added another 200,000 while estimatex of German casualties range between 250,000 and 600,000. Since the British were constantly attacking, it is not surprising that they may have lost two men for every casualty they inflicted on the enemy.

Given the Verdun situation, a British-led offensive in the Somme valley was inevitable in 1916. The operational challenge as envisioned by Haig himself was to fight the German Army in a cost-effective way and he failed to do this. British Prime Minister Herbert Asquith and his successor David Lloyd George lacked the determination or desire to replace Haig and historians too are sharply divided over his performance as Commander-in-Chief. For an overview see *Haig: A Re-Appraisal 80 Years On*. The most positive assessment is Gary Sheffield's *The Chief*.

Burial Ground at Somme. [CWM 19920085-749]

Battle of Vimy Ridge - 9 - 12 April 1917

Legend

German front - Apr. 9
Allied front - Apr. 9
German front - Apr. 12 - PM
German front - Apr. 13

Fresnoy
Arleux
Willerval
Farbus
Douai Plains
Thélus
Vimy
Lens
Vimy Ridge
Hill 145
The Pimple
Captured
6am, Apr 12
Souchez
Neuville-Saint-Vaast

10th Canadian
INF BDE
4th Division
3rd Division
2nd Division
1st Division
17th British
Corps

N

©2010 Google

VIMY AND THE ARRAS OFFENSIVE

HAIG'S POLICY OF CONTINUING the Somme battle after it was evident that there was little hope of defeating the enemy in 1916 was bitterly opposed by many British political leaders, including David Lloyd George who became Prime Minister in December 1916. Lloyd George's criticisms of Haig and the war of attrition on the Western Front would continue until the Armistice but in the absence of a convincing alternative strategy or better leaders the British and French armies were left alone to plan to renew the offensive in 1917.

Lloyd George was anxious to limit the slaughter in the trenches but he was not prepared to endorse the various peace proposals put forward by the American President, Woodrow Wilson, the Pope or the German government. The peace proposals of December 1916 were widely discussed in Britain and Canada. Since it was evident that negotiations were bound to produce a settlement favourable to Germany because of its occupation of important parts of France, most of Belgium, and large areas of the Russian empire, few individuals endorsed the idea of an Armistice in 1916. As there was no hope of peace on German terms, the Kaiser and his chief advisors decided to employ "unrestricted submarine warfare" as a means of ending Britain's capacity to continue the war. This policy, implemented in February 1917, led to the United States' declaration of war against Germany on 6 April 1917.

William Longstaff, Ghosts of Vimy Ridge. [CHOC Collection, (AN O-4714)]

Vimy Ridge Artillery Positions

0 1 2 3
kilometres

I British Corps

Front Lines Last Light 8 April

Cité de Caumont

Ablais-St. Nazaire

Souchez

The Pimple

Givenchy-en-Gohelle

Carency

Villers-au-Bois

4th Canadian Division

HILL 145

Canadian Corps

3rd Canadian Division

Neuville St. Vaast

Mont St. Eloi

2nd Can Div

1st Canadian Division

Maroeuil

Écurie

Arras

● Divisional artillery batteries
■ Medium batteries
▲ Heavy batteries
→ Super-heavy guns
— Narrow-gauge railways

N
W E
S

Throughout, allied military commanders remained committed to victory on the Western Front. The British preferred a plan to try and win control of the Belgian coast but agreed to cooperate with a French proposal for a coordinated Anglo-French attack designed to encircle and destroy large elements of the German Army. Before the "Nivelle offensive," named for the new French commander Robert Nivelle, began, the enemy withdrew to position known as the Hindenburg Line some 35 kilometres to the east. This manoeuvre destroyed what little prospect of success the plan had promised but the operation was not cancelled.

The British part in the April offensive, known as the Battle of Arras, included yet another attempt to capture Vimy Ridge, a feature which dominated the Lens-Douai plain to the east. The Germans did not abandon the ridge when they withdrew to the Hindenburg Line as the ground was considered of vital importance and the defences thought to be impenetrable. The Battle of Arras, like the rest of the 1917 spring offensive, yielded little beyond death and destruction, except at Vimy where the Canadian Corps, part of Henry Horne's First British Army, won an important local victory announced to the world as "Canada's Easter gift to France." The success of the Canadian Corps has given rise to a peculiar myth which relates the capture of Vimy Ridge to the emergence of Canada as a nation. This is a theme requiring analysis of the construction of post-war memory in English-speaking Canada rather than the actual events.

Canadian historians have also been drawn to the battle for Vimy Ridge when seeking to advance the idea that the Corps was a particularly effective component of the Allied armies. The first systematic study of these issues was Bill Rawling's

British tank crossing German trench at Vimy Ridge. All eight of the tanks available to the Canadians at Vimy broke down or were knocked out by enemy fire. [CWM 19930013-548]

Surviving Trench Warfare, which examined the changes in weapons and tactics between 1914 and 1918. Rawling argues that "each soldier" became "a specialist with a specific role to play in battle." The Canadian Corps, he writes, "moved away from the concept of a citizen-solider who would ride and shoot to an army of technicians, which, even in infantry battalions, specialized in particular aspects of fighting battles." Rawling believes that the growing sophistication of the Canadian Corps helps to explain the dramatic success at Vimy and in the battles of 1918.

Further study of the Vimy battle should begin with the essays in *Vimy Ridge: A Canadian Reassessment*. This collection, published by WLU Press with LCMSDS Press, provides a great deal of new information based on archival research while the critical reader is able to appreciate the very different perspectives of the seventeen contributors. Gary Sheffield, a British historian, believes the Canadian Corps is best understood as a fully integrated part of the Imperial Army. For Sheffield, a firm admirer of Field Marshal Haig, the entire British Expeditionary Force, not just the Canadians, was in the process of being transformed into "a large, sophisticated, technologically advanced and highly effective army."

Essays by Paul Dickson, Mark Humphries, Bill Rawling, and Tim Cook explore this process, and the book provides an account of the experience of each of the Canadian divisions at Vimy. This "learning curve" theme is further developed by Christopher Pugsley, a historian who has studied the Anzac experience. He stresses

In this nighttime photograph taken behind Canadian lines at Vimy Ridge, a British naval gun fires in support of the Canadian attack. Approximately 1,000 Allied guns and mortars pounded the ridge prior to the assault, a period called by the German defenders the "week of suffering." [CWM 19920085-215]

the debt the Australians and New Zealanders owed to the Canadian Corps. Puglsey believes that the Canadians led the way in re-organizing their rifle companies so that each of the four platoons (of 28 to 44 men) would include two sections of riflemen, who would also have rifle grenades, a section of Lewis guns to provide immediate covering fire and a bombing section armed with hand grenades. Puglsey credits Byng with implementing a standard platoon-focused battle doctrine in all four divisions of the Corps in December 1916. These changes, Puglsey suggests, were then implemented across the BEF beginning in February 1917.

Mark Humphries is less sure. He notes that the actual instructions issued by GHQ stressed the need to attack first in waves following the artillery barrage, then attacking the enemy with fixed bayonet. Platoon fire and movement tactics were reserved for situations where the normal advance was held up. None of this was particularly new, as one war diarist, quoted by Humphries, recorded "It will always be the work of the man with the rifle and bayonet to assault a position…the Lewis Gunner to resist a counterattack and support further advance, the bomber to mop up…."

There is much to be learned from these commentaries on the evolution of tactics, but Vimy was primarily a set-piece battle dominated by artillery. The troops were carefully rehearsed to move quickly to their assigned objectives relying on "one heavy gun for every 20 yards of front and a field gun for every ten yards, twice the density available at the Somme." This enormous firepower, most of it British, together with the elaborate counter-battery work of British and Canadian gunners permitted the Corps to move steadily across the sloping, featureless terrain. By early afternoon three of the four divisions had reached the crest of the ridge. When Hill 145, Fourth Division's objective which the French briefly held in May 1915, fell three days later the entire ridge was in Canadian hands. The Royal Flying Corps also played a major role in the Battle of Arras, obtaining air superiority and attacking the targets the Army requested. The cost, 275 aircraft and 421 casualties, was long remembered as "Bloody April" in the story of British airpower. The army's victory had also been costly—3,598 dead and 6,664 wounded—but the attack, Rawling argues, "ended with a different balance between costs and results."

Securing Vimy Ridge and thus protecting the left flank of Third Army's main effort, an advance to Cambrai was the major task assigned to the Canadian Corps and Henry Horne's First Army. Third Army, attacking with ten divisions plus infantry and cavalry reserves, captured all its initial objectives, the same Black, Brown and Blue lines seized by the Canadians at Vimy. Momentum was soon lost as the weather, casualties, exhaustion, and the arrival of German reserves stabilized the front a few miles beyond the start line. Both Third and First Armies demonstrated prowess at set-piece attacks, with massive amounts of artillery, but skill at breaking into the German defences did not lead to a break-through, never mind a break-out.

Canadian medical officers (with the Red Cross emblems on the soldiers at right and to the left rear of the photo) use German prisoners to help transport Canadian wounded from Vimy Ridge. They use a two-tiered carrier, pulled along a light railway line leading from the front. [CWM 19920085-924]

The capture of Vimy Ridge did not end Canadian participation in the Battle of Arras. The Nivelle offensive had been heralded as an action that could bring the war to an end but it began with heavy losses, 40,000 French casualties on the first day, and slight gains on the ground. Nivelle remained committed to the offensive and on 20 April began a determined assault on the Chemin des Dames Ridge that continued until 9 May. French losses were estimated at 187,000 men, German casualties reached a total of 168,000.

Haig would have preferred to cease operations in the Arras sector and move resources north for his long-planned offensive in Flanders, but the British were obliged to assist Nivelle by maintaining pressure on the Arras front. On 23 April, ten British divisions launched what is known as the Second Battle of the Scarpe. On 28 April, a second attempt to breach the German defences with six divisions including First Canadian was launched. Michael Bechthold who has studied these actions closely notes that Currie, still commanding the First Division, insisted on a two stage operation with an emphasis on planning to defeat German counterattacks. The Canadian success at Arleux was the only bright note on a day in which other divisions failed to make even limited gains.

On 3 May Haig began another attempt to reach the Drocourt-Quéant line employing fourteen divisions in the Third Battle of the Scarpe. "There were," Bechthold writes, "only two small successes... The First Anzac (Australian and New

Zealand Army Corps) captured Bullecourt and First Canadian Division captured and held Fresnoy." British historian J.P. Harris writes "The capture of Fresnoy was the culminating point of a series of brilliant successes by the Canadian Corps during the Arras battles and the relieving feature of a day which many who witnessed it consider the blackest day of the war." The "blackest day," so named because of heavy casualties and growing recognition that any further attempts to break the Hindenburg Line were unlikely to succeed.

Haig was now planning to switch the main British effort to the Ypres front but he believed that he had to continue operations in the Arras sector to mislead the enemy. For the Canadians this meant attacking in the Souchez-Avion sector in May and the implementation of a new policy of heavy raids designed to inflict casualties but not gain ground in June. Then on 7 July, as the build-up for the Flanders offensive continued, Haig ordered First Army to increase the scale of these diversionary attacks.

By this time, Byng's successful leadership of the Canadian Corps had won him promotion to command of Third Army crating a vacancy at the head of the Corps. The Borden government was insistent that a Canadian be given command of a formation that had become a source of pride and a status symbol for Canadians. The logical choice was Major-General Arthur Currie, First Canadian Division's able commander. Currie was not a professional soldier, but was a real estate salesman and sometime teacher living in Victoria, British Columbia at the outbreak of the war. He had made some questionable decisions as a brigadier at the Second Battle of Ypres, but thereafter had proved himself to be Canada's best general and one of Byng's most trusted commanders. Currie also had a secret past. In 1914, there had been a slump in real estate prices out west and Currie found himself in significant debt and

Canadians celebrate after the capture of Vimy Ridge. [PA 001353]

Aided by two Nursing Sisters, a wounded Canadian who took part in the August 1917 Battle of Hill 70 prepares to board a Red Cross train at a casualty clearing station. [CWM 19920085-704]

so he used his position as the commanding officer of a Victoria militia regiment to steal $10,000 in regimental funds to pay his creditors before attesting to go overseas. Few people knew about the potential scandal and it became a weight around the new corps commander's neck over the next few years—especially when his friend turned enemy, Sam Hughes, inexplicably refused to use the information publically. All this makes Currie a very human and no less gifted battlefield commander. He took command of the Corps on 9 June and was quickly confronted with an outline plan for a frontal assault on the coal mining centre of Lens. Currie studied the plan and came to the conclusion that as the operational goal was to draw in German reserves, instead of moving on the town itself which would be a costly undertaking, he should seize the bare chalk rise north of the city, known for its height in metres as Hill 70. This position dominated the ground to the east and could be carefully defended against the inevitable German counterattacks—it was a similar plan to what Falkenhayn had proposed to do at Verdun the previous year. Horne agreed to Currie's innovative proposal.

Continuous rain postponed the Hill 70 operation until 15 August when the First and Second Divisions, each with two brigades forward, attacked and captured the first and second German position on the crest of the hill. They then took sections of the Green line on the eastern reverse slope. A diversionary attack by 4th Canadian Division further disorganized the enemy who failed to appreciate the commanding view of the battlefield now in Canadian hands. Successive, poorly organized counterattacks were destroyed by observed artillery fire and machine guns. By 18 August the enemy was forced to concede the hill.

Unfortunately, Currie was buoyed by this first resounding success and he decided to ignore his earlier instincts and press on with an attack on Lens itself, which was slated to begin on 21 August. Both Second and Fourth Divisions were committed to an advance into the ruined city and both suffered significant losses before the confused affair was called off on the 25th. In the meantime, the Canadians had suffered 4,000 casualties between 21 and 25 August but were unable to hold any of their objectives in the city. A renewed attack was ordered for September but was cancelled when the Canadians were ordered north to join the battle for Passchendaele Ridge. Andrew Godefroy has edited a collection of essays titled *Great War Commands: Historical Perspectives on Canadian Army Leadership 1914-1918* that offers interesting background on Currie, Turner, and other senior Canadian commanders. The most recent study of Currie's life, focusing on his relationship with Sam Hughes, is Tim Cook's *The Madman and the Butcher*. Mark Humphries' *The Selected Papers of Sir Arthur Currie* provides a brief introduction to the general's life and provides readers with his letters and diaries.

Passchendaele - 22 October - 6 November 1917

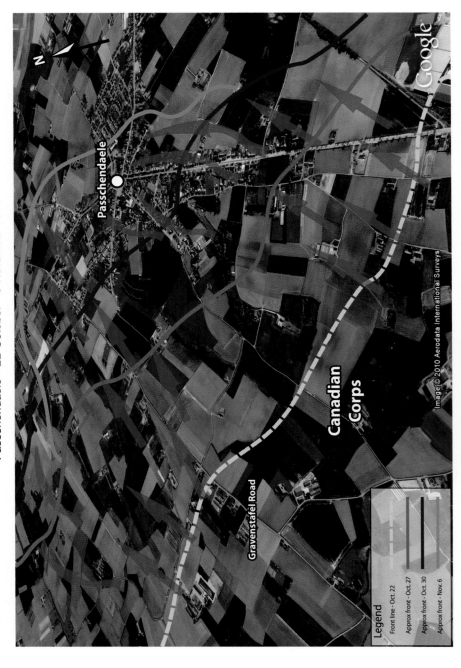

Passchendaele

Gravenstafel Road

Canadian
Corps

Image © 2010 Aerodata International Surveys

Google

Legend

Front line - Oct. 22

Approx front - Oct. 27

Approx front - Oct. 30

Approx front - Nov. 6

PASSCHENDAELE 1917

BY EARLY MAY 1917, as the Arras offensive was winding down, British and French politicians and Generals met in Paris to plan future action. Robert Nivelle had been fired and Philippe Pétain had become Chief of the General Staff. Pétain knew there was a growing morale crisis in the French Army, though the first signs of mutiny were still a month away. He made it clear that if further offensive action was planned for 1917 it would have to be carried out by the British Army. Haig made the case for a Flanders offensive aimed at clearing the Belgian coast. The Chief of the Imperial General Staff Sir William Robertson and the politicians accepted this proposal but Robertson, long an advocate of a step by step approach declared:

> It is no longer a question of aiming at breaking through the enemy's front and aiming at distant objectives. It is now a question of wearing down and exhausting the enemy's resistance ... relentlessly attacking with limited objectives and making the fullest use of our artillery. By this means we hope to gain our ends with the minimum loss possible.

No one present at the meeting addressed the contradiction between Robertson's caution and Haig's ambitious plans. His orders for a major operation on the Ypres front, with the object of securing the Belgian coast and advancing to the Dutch frontier were issued on 2 May. The outline plan called for a two-stage attack: to secure

Douglas Culham, "Mud Road to Passchendaele." [CWM 19890222-001]

the Messines Ridge in early June, and begin the more ambitious campaign in July.

The Messines Ridge which overlooked Ypres from the south east was one of the most thoroughly defended positions on the Western Front. It was, however, subject to observed artillery fire from still higher ground and vulnerable to underground attack by tunnelling companies. On 7 June 1917, nineteen mines were exploded under the ridge, destroying and demoralizing the defenders. A rapid British advance behind a creeping barrage followed. Six hours later the entire ridge was in British hands. Operational plans called for a further advance but German reserves and especially their artillery restored the front. Messines was a significant British victory.

The battle's most obvious lesson was that limited attacks with defined objectives had a greater chance of success than the type of unlimited offensive which Haig was now planning for Passchendaele, but the Commander-in-Chief continued to believe that an aggressive assault in Flanders might achieve the impossible: a breakthrough. By this point in the war, he had become convinced that his plan for a two stage battle (attrition followed by annihilation) was close to achieving success. The Somme, he argued retrospectively, had achieved its "objective" by denuding the German Army of irreplaceable manpower and so he urged a sceptical British War Cabinet to concentrate energies on the Western Front because, "Germany was within six months of total exhaustion of her available manpower if fighting continues at its present intensity." Of course, Haig had made a similar argument in July and again in September 1916 but this was forgotten. The Commander-in-Chief reassured the politicians that he had no intention of entering into a continuous offensive with heavy losses, but no one asked how this could be assured if fighting was to go on at its "current intensity."

A Canadian field gun bombarding enemy lines. The shells stacked to the left represent just a fraction of what would have been fired during a heavy bombardment. [NAS (186) X.25018]

Passchendaele, before and after the battle.

Meanwhile, the Germans used the lull between Messines and the main offensive to add defensive lines and strong points, including positions on Passchendaele Ridge. With nine German divisions available there was no apparent lack of manpower.

The British assault divisions trained and rehearsed as they had before the Vimy-Arras offensive and much attention was paid to the tactics to be employed by the remodelled platoons. Air superiority provided a detailed knowledge of the enemy and his gun positions, greatly assisting counter-battery planning. The bombardment began on 16 July. Two weeks later eleven divisions went over the top along an eight mile front. Hubert Gough, the Army Commander, believed a 4,000 to 5,000 yard advance was possible on the first day and planned accordingly, diluting the firepower available for the initial phase.

The first day of Third Ypres, 31 July, produced gains of up to 2,000 yards and 27,000 British casualties. The German counterattacks were defeated and the steady rain, which was to continue through most of August, hampered movement and contributed to the failure of British attacks launched on 10, 16 and 19 August.

Haig and Gough were sharply criticized for the failure of the August battles but no one had the courage to challenge Haig's argument that "final victory might be won by December" if more manpower and guns could be found. After a lengthy pause for the ground to dry and reinforcements to be trained, nine divisions, including I ANZAC Corps, mounted a major attack to gain control of the Passchendaele Ridge.

An advance of 1,200 yards at a cost of 21,000 casualties ought to have brought the Flanders offensive to a close, but again Haig persisted and a further 15,000 casualties were suffered in the capture and holding of Polygon Wood.

German losses were also heavy and Haig believed "decisive results were now possible." On 4 October, twelve divisions attacked seizing deliberately limited objectives. This action, known as Broodseinde, was seen as a great ANZAC success, but before other such attacks could be prepared the autumn rains began in earnest. The battlefield was transformed into a quagmire.

Despite the extraordinary conditions, further attacks were ordered. On 9 October the British and Australians suffered 15,000 casualties in a failed attempt to secure Passchendaele Ridge. If the Flanders offensive was to continue, fresh troops had to be found, and Haig decided that the Canadians who had been brought north to exploit success must instead fight in the sucking mud of Flanders to secure Passchendaele village.

There is a pervasive myth, fostered by Currie himself after the war, that he protested when the Canadians were ordered to Flanders and that he personally set the terms of the engagement only after an impassioned personal plea from Haig. In reality, although Canadians were proud of their "national army", the Canadian Corps was still just one part of the much larger BEF and was never an autonomous entity. After the battle, Currie maintained that he had tried to keep the Corps out of Flanders, but there is no contemporary evidence for this, or for stories about Haig visiting his headquarters to persuade Currie to agree. Haig's diary mentions

The mud at Passchendaele slowed all movement to a crawl, and left advancing troops exposed to enemy fire for longer periods of time during attacks. [CWM 19930013-512]

the Canadian distain for General Gough that had developed at the Somme, but the decision to attach the Canadians to Plumer's Second Army was taken before Currie even learned that his men were going north to Flanders. Neither it nor Currie's diary makes any suggestion of further hesitations.

As reluctant as the Canadians may have been, they arrived in Ypres two weeks before they attacked towards the ridge. Confronted with an endless expanse of water-filled shell craters and the detritus of months of a brutal conflict including unburied bodies, Currie was determined to stage a carefully controlled artillery-based battle advancing on the ridge in a series of short bounds. The first advance on 26 October was successful in that the Canadians dug in 500 yards beyond their start line. Neither the Australians on their right nor the British on the left were able to keep pace. The second phase began on 30 October and the Canadians moved onto the ridge taking the ruins of Passchendaele on 6 November. This placed them in a deeper salient subject to continuous German fire which added to the casualty toll already above 12,000 for the two week battle.

Currie and a number of historians include Passchendaele in the list of Canadian victories because it brought the long campaign to a conclusion, but there was little glory to be found in Flanders in 1917. Passchendaele may have been captured, but again there was no breakthrough, no role for the cavalry, and no landings on the Channel coast. The German Army was also clearly not exhausted. The best overall account of the battle is to be found in Prior and Wilson *Passchendaele: The Untold Story*. For the Canadian experience consult Tim Cook's *Shock Troops*.

Lieutenant Alfred Theodore Joseph Bastien, "Canadian Gunners in the Mud, Passchendaele." [CWM 19710261-0093]

A war-weary and muddied Canadian returns alone from the front. [CWM 19920085-028]

o·1027

CAMBRAI 1917

THE CANADIAN CORPS, WHICH had suffered more than 16,000 casualties during its brief tour in the mud of Flanders, was not involved in the battle of Cambrai, 20 November 1917, but the Canadian Cavalry Brigade and the Royal Newfoundland Regiment were in the heat of the action. The idea for a new offensive developed within Byng's Third Army which was holding the sector south of Arras, an area which had not been subjected to massive destruction. By combining predicted artillery fire with massed groups of tanks to overcome barbed wire that otherwise could only be cut by extended shelling, Byng hoped to achieve surprise, pierce the Hindenburg Line and pass the cavalry through the breach to roll up the German front.

This scheme, which reflected Byng's background as a cavalry officer, was far too ambitious and after initial and dramatic success, celebrated in England by ringing of church bells, the offensive ground to a halt. The troops of Third Army found themselves in a deep salient, ill-prepared for the inevitable German counterattacks.

The 29th Division, including the Newfoundland Regiment, was held in reserve until the Hindenburg Line was broken; it then moved forward seizing Masnières, Nine Wood and Marcoing. The Canadian Cavalry Brigade, attached to the 5th British Cavalry Division followed up the advance and during the afternoon a squadron of the Fort Garry Horse while in the lead found a crossing of the St. Quentin Canal, captured a German gun battery, and scattered a German infantry battalion in a dramatic charge, which won a Victoria Cross for Lieutenant Harcus Strachan who lived to receive the award.

British historian Simon Robbins, in his book *British Generalship on the Western Front*, concludes that during the period 1915-1917, the "undue optimism of the higher command was one of the direct causes of failure." The planning process was "too ambitious with the result that in nearly every major operation in France the irrepressible optimism of the Higher Formations carried on the offensive beyond the point when...it had ceased to show a profit because they never knew when to take their profit and stop." Above all else, though, Haig failed to grasp the fact that although suffering from much distress, the Germans were far from collapsing during 1916 and 1917 although strategically on the defensive.

The German Offensives
March to July 1918

N
W — E
S

Dunkirk

Calais

Franco-Belgian forces

Ghent

Second Army

Roulers

Lys

BELGIUM

Boulogne

Second German Offensive
9–29 April 1918

Hazebrouck

Merville

Robecq

First Army

Bailleul

Ypres

Passchendaele

Messines

Comines

Armentières

Estaires

Festubert

Béthune

Givenchy

La Bassée

Escaut

Aubin-St-Vaast

St.Pol

Tinques

Mont-St-Eloi

Lens

Vimy Ridge

Acheville

Arleux

Oppy

Gavrelle

Douai

Scarpe

Arras

Doullens

Third Army

Bapaume

Canal du Nord

British Sector

Albert

Somme

Clery

Péronne

First German Offensive
21 March to 4 April 1918

Amiens

Villers-Bretonneux

Avre

Moreuil

Chaulnes

St.Quentin

Fifth Army

FRANCE

Roye

Montdidier

Noyon

Chauny

La Fère

Crépy

Laon

Fourth German Offensive
9–13 June 1918

Compiègne

Aisne

Soissons

Sixth Army

Oise

Third German Offensive
27 May to 4 June 1918

Reims

French Sector

Château Thierry

Marne

Epernay

Fifth German Offensive
15–17 July 1918

Seine

PARIS

0   1   2   3
miles

THE GERMAN SPRING OFFENSIVE 1918

THE ATTRITIONAL BATTLES OF 1917, which led to mutinies within the French Army, seriously weakened the British and Commonwealth forces on the Western Front. All indices of declining morale, including desertion rose significantly. Censorship reports on soldiers letters noted a lack of confidence in senior commanders and a growing belief that the war could not be won. Then in the winter of 1918, collapse of the Russian armies and the negotiations that ended in the Treaty of Brest-Litovsk allowed the Germans to transfer a large number of divisions from the Eastern Front, increasing the likelihood of a major German offensive in the spring. As Haig told the War Cabinet, the whole British Army is "exhausted and much reduced in strength." The only divisions "fit for duty" in the front line are "those belonging to the Australian and Canadian Corps."

Since the beginning of the war, Canadian manpower had been sustained by volunteers, but by the end of the fighting at Arras in the spring of 1917, the Borden government moved to bring in compulsory military service, or conscription, to address the growing shortfall in replacements for the front. That summer and during a bitter December election, Wilfrid Laurier's Liberals opposed the new Union Government's attempts to enforce the Military Service Act drawing finding support in Quebec as well as rural Canada and amongst new immigrants from non-English speaking countries. Thanks in no small part to the Military Voters Act, which extended the franchise to women with an immediate relative overseas, disenfranchised so-called "enemy aliens," and allowed the government to redistribute hundreds of thousands of soldiers' votes to hotly contested ridings, Borden prevailed. Although conscription created a new source of manpower, the first draftees would not arrive in France until the following summer.

Despite the Dominion's manpower crisis, the Canadians were far better off than their British counterparts. Declining enlistments in England forced the British Army to reduce the size of the each of its divisions from twelve to nine battalions, and even then many units had to remain under strength. The Canadians, Australians and New Zealanders were able to retain larger establishments marking the Australian and Canadian Corps as the strongest formations in the BEF. Consequently, the British War Office wanted the Canadians to organize two corps totalling six smaller divisions, but Currie argued for strengthening his powerful four-division corps and told Prime Minister Borden that it would be a mistake to break-up what many had come to see as Canada's national army. Instead, he suggested breaking up Fifth Canadian Division that was training in England under the command of Garnet Hughes, both to provide reinforcements and as a source for his plans to provide the corps with additional artillery, engineers and infantry reserves sufficient to supply each battalion with one hundred extra men. Borden agreed with Currie's assessment and, anxious to avoid having to resupply six full divisions with ancillary troops, informed the British that the Canadian Corps would remain as it was. As a result, throughout 1918 the Canadian Corps was the most powerful corps in the BEF, twice as strong as a normal British Corps of three divisions.

By February 1918, the British and Dominion divisions were struggling to build defences along a 123-mile front in anticipation of a major German offensive, ineptly copying German plans for mounting a defence in depth on an extended line. The enemy struck on 21 March, attacking on both sides of the Somme against the Third and Fifth British Armies. The Germans had seventy-eight divisions available for the spring of 1918 with specially selected storm trooper formations to lead Operation Michael, the first of three major operations. Initially Michael was successful especially against Fifth Army in the sector south of the Somme. Brigadier Raymond Brutinel's First Canadian Motor Machine Gun Brigade was dispatched south to assist Fifth Army and during the retreat towards Amiens, forty armoured cars saw action for nineteen consecutive days. Seventy-five percent of the brigade's combat troops became casualties, but they played a significant role in slowing the German advance.

The Canadian Cavalry Brigade was also committed in the Amiens front providing a dismounted force of 800 men to help defend the Crozat Canal and assist in the withdrawal of British forces from the area. The Canadian brigade's moment of glory came on 29 March when the Royal Canadian Dragoons, Fort Garry Horse and Lord Strathcona's Horse fought the battle of Moreuil Wood in defence of the ancient cathedral city.

On 28 March, the Germans launched their second operation code-named Mars at the boundary between First and Third Armies. The Second Canadian Division

Alexander Young, Cite Jeanne D'arc; "Hill 70 in the Distance." [CWM 19710261-018]

had come under command of Third Army on 27 March as did First Division the following day. Second Division was involved in Third Army's defensive battle south of Arras, repelling local attacks and staging raids on the Germans. The division did not return to the Canadian Corps until 1 July.

Currie also lost control of his other two divisions leading him to protest that this was tactically unsound as well as contrary to Canadian government policy. Currie carried his protests to England where Sir Edward Kemp, the Canadian Cabinet Minister for Overseas Services, pressured the British Government to meet Currie's wishes. Haig was to complain that "some people in Canada regard themselves as 'allies' rather than fellow citizens in the Empire" and he contrasted the cooperative attitude of the ANZACs with the attitude of the Canadians. Currie's protests had no immediate effect as Canada was not an ally but a part of a larger British Army and the Canadian Corps was only reformed once the German spring offensives finally collapsed in anticipation of a counter-stroke. Yet one unintended but important consequence of Canadian resistance was that by limiting the Corps' role during the spring offensive to the defence of the Vimy-Lens area, the Canadian formation was the only unbloodied unit in the BEF when it came time to hit back at the weakened German Army.

The final German offensive in Flanders, "Georgette," began on 9 April and forced the British to abandon Passchendaele Ridge and retire from Armentières. With thirty-one divisions available, the German Fourth Army appeared to be overwhelming the thirteen British and French divisions in the sector and Haig issued his famous "backs to the wall" order. Fortunately, Flanders mud, logistics and the determination of the defenders stopped the German advance at the edge of Ypres.

The Germans had not achieved a breakthrough and had suffered terrible losses, but so had the British. The German decision to focus the next attack in the south on the French Army at the Chemin des Dames was a desperate attempt to catch the Entente forces, which were now jointly commanded by French General Ferdinand Foch, on an uneven footing. The final offensive, code-named "Blucher," began on 27 May and continued until 18 July when the French Army mounted the first great counter-offensive known as the Second Battle of the Marne, an action that spelled the end of German ambitions to win the war in the west.

As Holger Herwig argues in *The First World War: Germany and Austria-Hungary 1914-1918*, the German offensives of 1918 were a gamble that failed. By the beginning of August the German Army in the West had suffered close to one million casualties and needed to defend an additional 100 kilometres of front line. Worse, they had traded their carefully fortified defensive zone for hastily prepared positions with little depth. Morale problems and the rapid spread of influenza, which affected the German Army before the virus reached the Allied armies, further weakened the Kaiser's forces.

Battle of Amiens - 8-11 August 1918

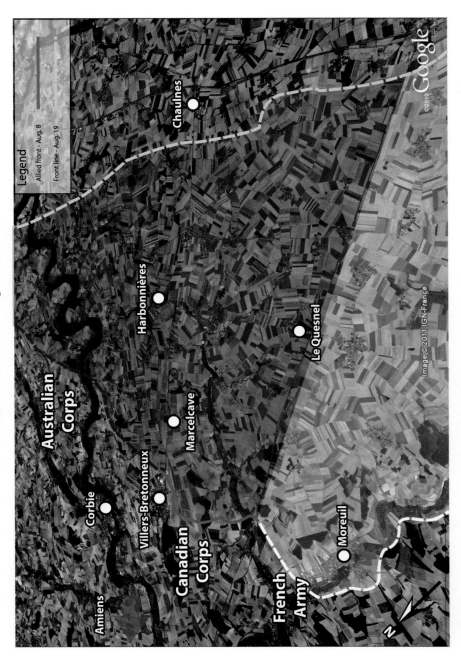

Legend

Allied front - Aug. 8

Front line - Aug. 19

Chaulnes

Harbonnières

Le Quesnel

Australian
Corps

Marcelcave

Corbie

Villers-Bretonneux

Canadian
Corps

Amiens

Moreuil

French
Army

N

Google

©2010

Image ©2011 IGN-France

THE BATTLE OF AMIENS

ENTENTE LEADERS BEGAN TO prepare a second major counter-offensive in the Somme valley, but the operational plan was influenced by the Australian success at Le Hamel, a village east of Amiens. General Sir John Monash, the aggressive Australian Corps commander, had attacked without any preliminary bombardment using forty tanks to support his infantry division (with an American battalion) to capture the position in just 40 minutes.

Le Hamel served as a model for Rawlinson, the commander of Fourth Army, who planned an attack at Amiens that was initially intended only to relieve the main north–south railway line that linked the French and British armies from German pressure. Rawlinson was given the Canadian Corps so that, with the Australians, the two strongest corps in the BEF could lead the attack. All four Canadian divisions were secretly brought south during the first days of August, which Shane Schreiber argues was a triumph of staff work in *Shock Army of the British Empire.*

The main battle was fought on the Plaine du Santerre, an area of "vast fields of wheat, barley and oats interspersed with orchards and brick-walled villages… ideal ground… for tank and infantry co-operation." North of the Somme, British Third Corps faced much more complex terrain with a succession of ridges to be overcome.

A team of over 30 soldiers pull a 60-pounder gun out of the gun line during the Battle of Amiens in 1918. [CWM 19930012-427]

A German observation post camouflaged as a tree trunk on the Arras-Lens road [CWM 19920085-829]

The XXXI Corps (French First Army) was to advance in step with the Canadians protecting their right flank. Brutinel's "Independent Force," composed of two Motor Machine Gun Brigades, maintained contact with the French using its mobility to great advantage.

The battle was an army-level operation and could only succeed through co-operation especially between the Australians and Canadians. Allied intelligence reports described the ten German divisions in the battle zone as weak and thinly spread—documents captured from enemy headquarters during the attack reveal that German battalions were in some cases at only a quarter strength. For once, intelligence proved accurate. Amiens is often remembered as a tank battle as Fourth Army's order of battle included 324 of the new Mark V and 96 Mark A "Whippet" tanks. Each Canadian division was allotted a battalion of 36 heavy tanks plus six Mark IV supply tanks. Additional supply tanks were made available to support the engineers.

As with all battles on the Western Front, artillery played a principal role. Over 2,000 guns supported the attack, 646 for the 8.5 kilometre front attacked by the Canadians. The attempt to achieve surprise meant no preliminary bombardment and no opportunity to register guns for counter-battery. At 0420 hours on 8 August the Australians and Canadians moved forward against a startled enemy beaten down by a hurricane of high explosive. Early morning mist helped to add tactical to operational surprise.

The Second Canadian Division's first major obstacle was the fortified village of Marcelcave. The 4th Brigade, which was to lead the attack, had been under artillery fire for more than an hour when the Allied barrage began. The 28 Mark V tanks available assisted the infantry advance but Marcelcave could only be entered after "a punishing forty-five minute artillery bombardment reduced much of the village to rubble." The remaining German soldiers forced the Canadians into a battle for the ruins before the advance could continue. Good co-operation between 7th Australian Brigade and the Canadians assisted both brigades in the rapid penetration of the "Green Line" which was secure by 0745, less than four hours after the advance began. The 5th Brigade then took over the Canadian advance, reaching the "Red Line" by early afternoon. Major-General Henry Burstall committed 6th Brigade to the final phase, the occupation of the "Blue Line" which was won before dark.

In the centre, First Canadian Division had run into strong resistance at Hangard Woods where enemy machine guns, well protected by barbed wire, required extraordinary efforts by small groups of men. Two Victoria Crosses were awarded in this action, Private John Croak and Corporal H. Good both of the 13th (Black Watch) Battalion. Once through the crust, First Division reached the "Blue Line" by early evening.

Major-General L.J. Lipsett's Third Division faced the most challenging tasks. The lead brigade was to advance along the main Amiens-Roye road which was naturally well defended. The French Corps on their right flank employed an hour-long artillery barrage before attacking and this obviously could not begin until the Canadian advance was underway. Fortunately, Brutinel's force acted swiftly, protecting the exposed flank. The division's left flank straddled the River Luce which was bordered by marshes, making much of it impassable. This terrain feature forced Lipsett to employ two brigades with 9th Brigade committed to an exceptionally narrow front south of the river. Their first task: cleaning "Rifle" or "Dodo" Woods.

The 43rd Battalion (Cameron Highlanders) and the 94th French Infantry Regiment co-operated closely in this action creating an international company composed of a platoon from each army to assist the attack. Canadian engineers played a crucial role in maintaining momentum, repairing bridges and building pontooned cork footbridges across the marshy Luce valley.

North of the river, Third Division's 8th Brigade cleared Hangard Woods and captured the village. The 7th Brigade, in reserve, advanced along the main road behind a new barrage designed to bring them to the Red Line. Despite gas shells and cratered ground they reached their objective, dug in and watched in amazement as the Third Cavalry Division with the Canadian Brigade in the lead came forward to test the long-promised chances of a breakout. The "Whippet" tanks, in support, proved too slow for the cavalry and German machine guns cut down horses and riders. The Canadian brigade lost 245 men in a series of "gallant but futile charges."

Canadians wounded at the Battle of Amiens lying outside of the 10th Field Ambulance Dressing Station. German prisoners of war are also dispersed through the crowd. [CWM 19930012-404]

Six Canadian infantry soldiers rest in a shell hole during the Battle of Amiens in 1918. [CWM 19930012-407]

Elsewhere, the cavalry enjoyed some success, one regiment intercepting a trainload of reinforcements and taking 600 prisoners.

Ironically, the success at Amiens came somewhat unexpectedly, although Currie had placed the Fourth Canadian Division in position to exploit whatever success his infantry and the Third Calvary Division obtained. Haig and Rawlinson now believed that the Amiens-Roye road was the best axis of advance. The Germans were equally committed to defending the sector and despite the commitment of fresh troops the enemy held a key Canadian objective, Le Quesnel, (where the Canadian Memorial for the Amiens battle is located) against repeated attacks. Le Quesnel fell the next morning, but the strength of the German defence pointed to a significant change in the rhythm of the battle. The Canadians had advanced 13 kilometres, a distance unprecedented on the Western Front but there was no breakthrough. Despite a further advance of up to 3 kilometres on 9 August it was becoming evident that German reinforcements, nine additional divisions by 10 August, were closing off the chances of reaching Péronne or Roye. Just 38 tanks were available across the entire Fourth Army front and the Allied soldiers were exhausted. Currie and other commanders sought to persuade Haig to call off the offensive. Currie was not just a highly successful commander; he was also the head of Canada's national army. His written protest persuaded Haig to end the Amiens offensive. Sir Julian Byng's Third Army was to stage the next attack while the Canadians returned to First Army and the Arras sector to prepare for a major assault on the Hindenberg Line. You may wish to read J.P Harris, *Amiens to the Armistice* for background on the overall campaign as well as J.L. Granatstein's *The Greatest Victory*.

Arras and Breaking the DQ Line - 26 August - 2 September 1918

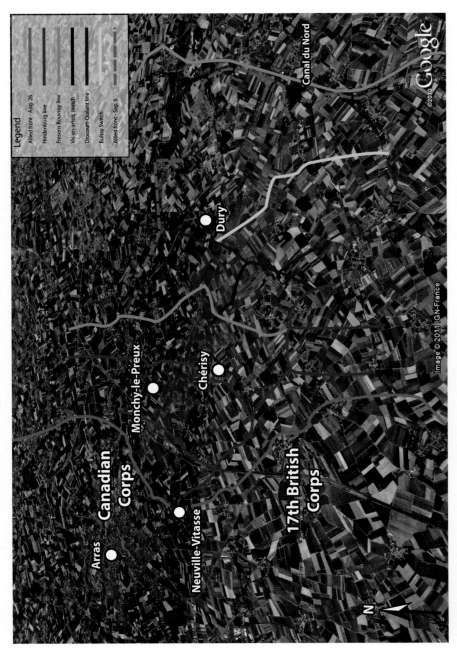

Legend

Allied front - Aug. 26
Hindenburg line
Fresnes-Rouvroy line
Vis-en-Artois switch
Drocourt-Quéant line
Buissy Switch
Allied front - Sep. 6

Canal du Nord

Dury

Monchy-le-Preux

Chérisy

Canadian Corps

Arras

Neuville-Vitasse

17th British Corps

N

©2010 Google

Image ©2011 IGN-France

THE HUNDRED DAYS: ARRAS TO MONS 1918

WITH THE GERMAN ARMY reeling, Sir Julian Byng's Third Army began an advance north of the Somme towards Bapaume. Byng was hesitant, convinced that German reinforcements would block an Amiens-like penetration, so he adopted a bite and hold approach which proved effective. Pausing to consolidate after securing minor gains his British forces, plus the New Zealand Division, inflicted heavy casualties when the Germans counterattacked. The next day Third Army renewed the attack, overwhelming the defenders and taking 10,000 prisoners. Known as the "Battle of Albert" its success, coming on the heels of Amiens and Tenth French Army's five mile advance on the British flank, led Haig to send an extraordinary message to his army commanders. The enemy, he insisted, "has not the means to deliver counterattacks on an extended scale nor has he the numbers to hold a position against the very extended advance which is now be directed upon him" by all the Allied armies. "Risks which a month ago would have been criminal ought now to be incurred as duty." It was, Haig believed, the return of open warfare where divisions would act "independently of its neighbour advancing to distant objectives." At last, it seemed,

Alfred Theodore Joseph Bastien, "Cavalry and Tanks at Arras, 1918." [CWM 19710261-0090]

Crossing the Canal du Nord & Bourlon Wood - 27 September 1918

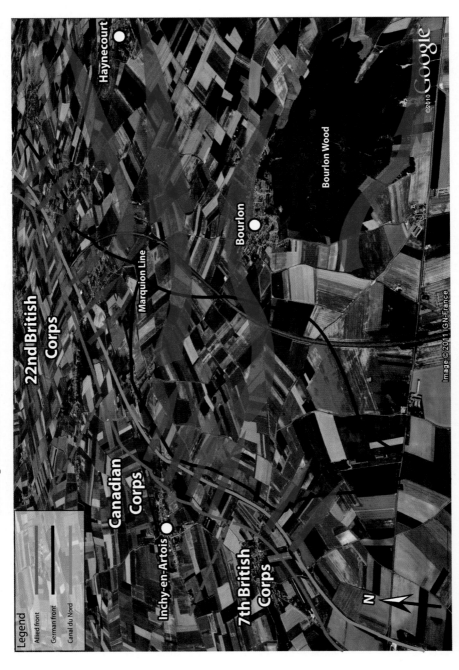

the German Army had been exhausted by four years of brutal, attritional warfare.

As the battlefield became more open, different tactics had to be employed although no experienced corps commander would cease to use his artillery as the principal weapon and none would order divisions to act independently. The dream of using the Cavalry Corps to gain "strategic objectives" remained just a fantasy. The great advance would be made by the poor bloody infantry.

Haig's orders now called for "an advance by all troops on all fronts" drawing Fourth Army back into combat. The Canadians were returning to Horne's First Army in the Arras sector so Rawlinson was left with III British Corps and the Australians. Between 24 August and 1 September the Australians led an advance that took them across the Somme and onto Mont St. Quentin hill north of Péronne that dominated the area. Péronne itself fell the next day.

The initial task assigned to the Canadian Corps was to overcome the German defences based on a series of hills. Historian Colonel G.W.L. Nicholson described the scene, which included the previously bloodied heights of Monchy-le-Preux:

> The enemy's main defence positions, supplemented by various subsidiary switches and strong points, were among the strongest on the Western Front. The ground was pocked with the scars of 1917 and early 1918, and in the litter of old trenches and fortifications German engineers had found ready-made positions which they had considerably strengthened. Furthermore, topography was on the side of the Germans. The battle area spread over the north-eastern slopes of the Artois Hills, whose summits about Monchy were over three hundred feet above the valley-bottoms of the Scarpe and the Sensée. The latter river, flowing generally eastward, together with its tributaries had dissected the hills into numerous deep valleys. The intervening ridges and high points, often mutually supporting, the enemy had fortified with a skill that demonstrated his mastery in military engineering.

Canadian supply units cross the dry bed of the Canal du Nord. [CWM 19930012-815]

Known as the Battle of the Scarpe, the operation began at 0300 hours 26 August 1918 with fourteen brigades of field artillery, and nine heavy brigades. There were few tanks available after the losses east of Amiens and just nine were allotted to each of the two divisions leading the attack.

North of the Arras-Cambrai road, the centre-line of the Corps advance, Third Canadian Division seized their first objectives in less than five hours. The division, commanded by Major-General L.J. Lipsell, a British officer of exceptional ability who had previously commanded 8th Battalion at Ypres and 2nd Brigade at Mount Sorrel, was confident enough to stage a complex night attack. The 8th Brigade with three battalions of the (dismounted) Canadian Mounted Rifles in the lead overcame the German defences at Orange Hill and the heights of Monchy-Le-Preux by outflanking the enemy and attacking from two directions.

The Second Division also made good initial progress but orders to shift the weight to the southeast, capturing the Wancourt Ridge, to assist Third Army slowed the advance to the division's objectives. After a night of heavy rain both Canadian divisions made some progress against determined opposition, advancing five miles while overcoming the remaining defences of the Fresnes-Rouvroy system. The actions cost the Canadians close to 6,000 men, a taste of what was to come at the Drocourt-Quéant or D-Q Line, one of the most formidable German positions.

Casualties to British and Dominion formations were now causing grave concern. The British War Cabinet sent a telegram to Haig (29 August) warning

German mortars captured during the Canal du Nord operation. One of the mortars has been marked by the 4th Battalion, which captured it on 27 September. From 22 August to 11 October 1918, the Canadians captured 371 guns and nearly 2,000 machine-guns. [CWM 20020045-2469]

against incurring heavy losses in the next weeks as infantry reinforcements for the BEF were simply not available. Due to the breakup of Fifth Canadian Division and the arrival of conscripts, the Canadians were the only one of Haig's Corps able to restore formations to full strength. This inevitably meant that Currie would be asked to take the lead in the next series of costly assaults. The situation was dramatized when Fourth British Division, which had fought under Currie in the second phase of the late August advance, reported that only one brigade was fit for action against the D-Q Line, forcing the Canadians to take an even larger share of the assault.

Breaking through the D-Q Line required detailed planning and lots of artillery. There was little opportunity for any kind of "open warfare." Five brigades following a rolling barrage would have to overcome three defensive lines before reaching the ground overlooking the Canal du Nord. Currie decided to attack at dawn hoping that the Mark V tanks could move forward with the infantry at zero hour. By the end of the day, seven Canadians had won the Victoria Cross and the D-Q Switch, as it was also known, had been breached on a 7,000 metre front. The next morning the enemy was gone, retreating behind the Canal du Nord. Over 6,000 German soldiers were in corps prisoner of war cages and many more were killed or wounded, at a cost of some 5,600 Canadian casualties.

The successful assault on the D-Q Line, the most complete defensive system on the Western Front, was supported by a parallel British-Australian advance to Bapaume, forcing a German retreat all along the front. The German withdrawal slowed the operational tempo, allowing the Canadians to rest, but Third British Army resumed the advance on 12 September and Fourth Army joined in six days later. On 25 September a large-scale Franco-American offensive on a 44-mile front began. The next day First Army was ordered to cross the Canal du Nord and seize Bourlon Wood. General Henry Horne, who commanded First Army, has been described as "a rather shadowy figure for historians ... eclipsed by the prominence given to Sir Arthur Currie, his Canadian subordinate." Horne seemed content to leave the planning and conduct of operations to Currie which meant the Canadians did most of the heavy lifting in First Army.

Currie decided to advance on a narrow front, less than 2,500 metres, where the Canal du Nord was under construction and still dry. The enemy had strengthened defences in the area with dense belts of barbed wire but there was little protection from the kind of bombardment corps and army artillery could apply. Beyond the canal, a second defensive position, the Marquion Line, crossed the front. The main objective, the high ground at Bourlon Wood, was to be attacked after the reserve brigades of Fourth Canadian Division had crossed the canal to add weight to the advance.

A massive creeping barrage mixing smoke, shrapnel and high explosive led

Battle of Cambrai - 28 September - 11 October 1918

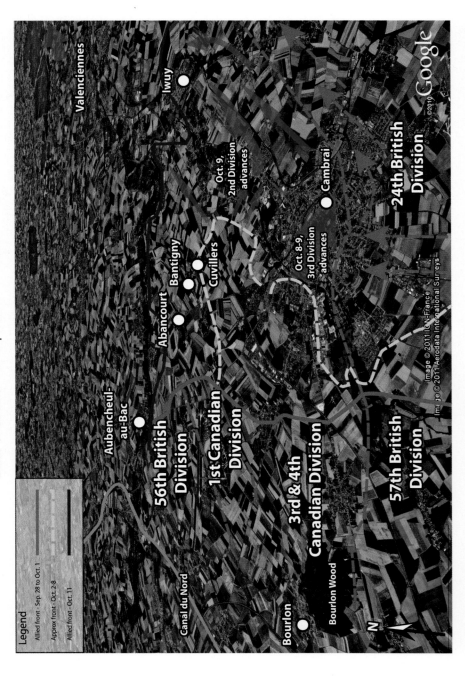

Legend

Allied front - Sep. 28 to Oct. 1
Approx front - Oct. 2-8
Allied front - Oct. 11

Valenciennes

Iwuy

Oct. 9,
2nd Division
advances

Cambrai

24th British
Division

Abancourt

Bantigny

Cuvillers

Oct. 8-9,
3rd Division
advances

Aubencheul-
au-Bac

56th British
Division

1st Canadian
Division

3rd & 4th
Canadian Division

57th British
Division

Canal du Nord

Bourlon

Bourlon Wood

N

Google

Image © 2011 IGN-France
Image © 2011 Aerodata International Surveys
©2019

the way. Although the German Armies had been depleted, machineguns situated in concrete pillboxes, along high railway embankments, and dense woods still did their damage. The country across which the Canadians had to advance was largely flat, open terrain which left the infantry vulnerable wherever German gunners had escaped the bombardment. For example, the 38th Battalion took heavy casualties when machine gunners firing from the railway line running north from Bourlon cut them to ribbons as they walked forward through the autumn fields. But despite such losses, once again the Canadians overwhelmed the defenders and in less than five hours Bourlon Wood was brought under attack. This heavily wooded hill above Bourlon village could well have been the scene of protracted battle since the ground and an open flank to the south combined to challenge the determination of David Watson's Fourth Canadian Division. One need only visit the quiet, hauntingly beautiful Bourlon Wood Cemetary, tucked away just past the Canadian hilltop memorial to find evidence of the cost. Fortunately the enemy withdrew to the Marcoing Line and Bourlon Wood was in Canadian hands by midnight on 28 September. Elsewhere air support and superb work by the engineers who bridged the canal helped to maintain momentum and by nightfall leading elements were probing the last fortified positions in front of Cambrai. Unfortunately the Germans were determined to hold the city and the Escaut canal and Marcoing line as long as possible. The battle for Cambrai turned into a bitter, attritional struggle.

After a failed attack by the Fourth Division, Currie ordered the Corps to stage a new set-piece attack on 1 October. After initial progress enemy resistance stiffened and then a series of German counterattacks forced a withdrawal. For the moment, the enemy had stabilized the front. Cambrai, badly damaged by shelling and arson, was finally cleared on 9 October after Third Army succeeded in crossing the canal

A small patrol of Canadian troops crosses the main square in Cambrai on 9 October 1918. The retreating Germans set fire to the town, but the rapid Canadian occupation allowed much of the city to be saved from the flames. [CWM 19900076-760]

Battle of Valenciennes - 1-11 October 1918

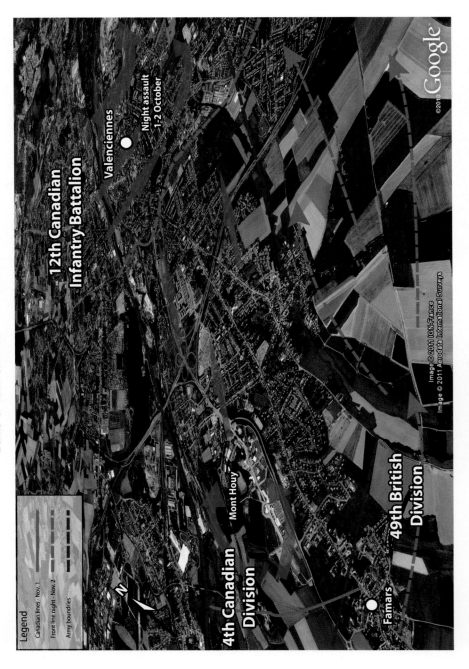

Legend
Canadian lines - Nov. 1
Front line night - Nov. 2
Army boundries

12th Canadian
Infantry Battalion

Valenciennes

Night assault
1-2 October

N

4th Canadian
Division

Mont Houy

49th British
Division

Famars

Image © 2011 IGN-France
Image © 2011 Aerodata International Surveys

Google
©2010

south of the city, threatening a double envelopment. The Canadians fought their way into Cambrai, overcoming rear guards and dealing with mines and booby-traps. On 11 October the Corps was sent into reserve. The summary offered by the official historian states:

> It's casualties were many but by First World War standards not excessive in light of their task. The total officially reported killed, wounded, and missing between 22 August and 11 October numbered 1,544 officers and 29,262 other ranks. In achieving its victory the Corps had captured 18,585 prisoners, together with 371 guns and nearly 2,000 machine guns. Besides depriving the enemy of the great distributing centre of Cambrai, the Canadians had liberated 54 towns and villages standing on more than 116 square miles of French soil.

Cambrai was a complex battle fought on the outskirts and eventually the streets of an industrial city. No historian has examined this operation in any detail – an important task for the future. From Cambrai the Corps advanced to Valenciennes and Mons in the last month of the war. The story of the final advance needs to be understood in the context of the German effort to achieve an Armistice which would preserve the Kaiser's regime, the prestige of the German Army, and as many territorial conquests as possible.

On 10 September, the German High Command agreed to permit an approach to the Allies through the Queen of the Netherlands. This gambit was abandoned when on 14 September the Austrian Emperor, fearing the complete disintegration of his armies, issued a public appeal for a peace conference in a neutral state. This transparent attempt to preserve a collapsing empire was followed by a public declaration of German war aims that called for preserving the Treaty of Brest-Litovsk, the return of all German colonies, and effective control of Belgium.

President Wilson's reply to the Austrian peace note included his enunciation of five essential conditions for peace, an elaboration of the famous "Fourteen Points." He added words that forced Germany's leaders to rethink their claims. Wilson declared "there can be no peace obtained by any bargain or compromise with the Governments of the Central Empires." The next day Bulgaria, one of the four Central Powers, surrendered. Ludendorff subsequently wrote that 28 September was the day he knew "the war was now lost...If we had the strength to reverse the situation in the West, then of course nothing would yet have been lost. But we had not the means… We had to count on being beaten back again and again."

Insisting that "every hour of delay is dangerous," Ludendorff led an effort to reconstitute the German government and issue an immediate call for an end to the fighting. A new Chancellor, Prince Max of Baden, was appointed on 4 October and "with a view to avoiding further bloodshed" he signed a letter to President Wilson requesting an immediate Armistice.

The Allied Advance
Jul–Nov 1918

GERMANY

LUXEMBOURG

BELGIUM

FRANCE

English Channel

Maastricht

Antwerp
Brussels
Namur
Charleroi

Ghent
Bruges
Ostend
Calais
Dieppe
Rouen

Lessines
Courtrai
Ypres
Hazebrouck
Armentieres
Lille
Tournai
Mons
Maubeuge
Avesnes
Valenciennes
Douai
Cambrai
Albert
Peronne
St. Quentin
Moreuil
Amiens

Sedan
Mezieres
Reims
Laon
Soissons

Namur

Metz
Mars la Tour
St. Mihiel
St. Dizier

front line 11 Nov
front line 18 July

front line 11 Nov
front line 18 July

Belgian/ French

British Second
British First (Canadian Corps)
British Third
British Fourth

French First
French Third until 14 Sep
French Sixth withdrawn 7 Sep
French Tenth until 27 Oct
French Third
French Fifth
French Ninth withdrawn 24 Jul
French Fourth
French Second/ US First from 22 Sep

US First from 9 Aug
US Second from 12 Oct
French Tenth/ French Eighth from 6 Nov

Schelde
Lys
Dendre
Zenne
Dyle
Sambre
Meuse
Somme
Oise
Aisne
Marne
Seine
Moselle
Meuse

0   25   50
miles

Wilson's reply, on 8 October, demanded immediate "withdrawal of their forces everywhere from invaded territory"–not the response the German government was hoping for. On 12 October the Germans agreed to evacuate occupied territory but with an international commission supervising the process.

Any chance of a conciliatory response from Wilson or other Allied leaders was diminished by the sinking of the Irish Mail Boat *RMS Leinster* on 10 October. Over 500 men, women, and children including soldiers returning from leave were drowned in this pointless U-boat attack. Wilson echoed the public outcry, insisting on 14 October that "there can be no peace as long as Germany attacks passenger ships." The small coterie of decision-makers in Germany remained divided and uncertain. Ludendorff wanted to avoid any responsibility for a military surrender while Crown Prince Rupprecht warned that "we must obtain peace before the enemy breaks through into Germany…."

Prince Max crafted a new note on 20 October accepting the need to have military advisors determine the details of the Armistice as long as no demands were made "that would be irreconcilable with the honour of the German people and with paving the way to a peace of justice." He did promise to end the sinking of passenger ships. Wilson then announced that the Entente and allied forces would not negotiate nor accept terms from the Kaiser who would have to abdicate if discussions were to lead to an armistice. This led to Ludendorff's resignation while the Kaiser fled into exile in Holland: there was nothing the German Army could do to dictate terms or stabilize the line. The war was effectively over.

The collapse of the German Army and the Imperial state was remarkably swift. The German people had been starved of both food and reliable information for four years. The previous winter had been known as the turnip winter when most supplies of grain, meat, and fat had disappeared. German newspapers had convinced a highly literate and patriotic population that the war could still be won so long as the spring offensives went as planned and so they persevered. News of the defeats that summer and fall had been kept secret and so the collapse of the German Army seemed inexplicable so that rioting and socialist uprisings inspired by the Bolshevik Revolution the previous year in Russia quickly swept across the country, feeding off the hunger and anger of the people. As Ludendorff left his post, he also attempted to deflect blame from himself and the German generals who had kept the war going for so long after any hope of victory had disappeared: the German Army had not actually been defeated in the field, he argued, for it had been stabbed in the back by the socialist politicians and revolutionary's at home who agreed to form a provisional government in the Kaiser's absence. This laid the groundwork for the *Dolchstoss* myth that would be so effectively exploited and expanded by Adolf Hitler

Mons - 11 November 1918

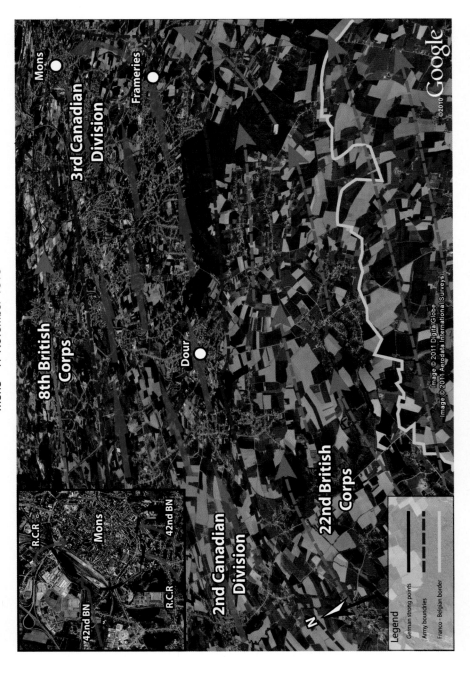

and the Nazi Party in the post-war period. There is no question, though, that the German Army had been defeated on the battlefield as indicated by their acceptance of the Armistice a few days later. The collapse of the German state was a direct result of the decision-making of the Kaiser and his Great General Staff.

Neither the British nor the French governments had finalized a decision on the exact terms of an Armistice and soon events made such discussion irrelevant. The Turkish Government sent envoys to sign a separate peace on 26 October and Austria soon followed. On 5 November Marshal Ferdinand Foch was authorized to "receive representatives of the German Government and communicate to them the terms of the Armistice." The terms were presented on 8 November in a railway carriage in the Forêt de Compiègne, north of Paris. The German delegates were given 22 hours until 1100 hours on 11 November to sign the Armistice.

The prolonged Armistice negotiations had little impact on Allied military operations raising the age-old question of the legitimacy or wisdom of continuing combat when the war is all but won. This issue became particularly important to Canadians after Sir Arthur Currie was later criticized for the unnecessary deaths of Canadian soldiers in the final hours of the war. Rumours, innuendo and specific attacks on his reputation by Sam Hughes, during and after the war, culminated in the famous trial in Port Hope where Currie defended his reputation and won a form of vindication in 1928.

Currie consistently argued that the Canadian Corps had been following explicit orders as it advanced towards Mons in the last week of the war. Certainly the last

Frederick Varley, "For What?" [CWM 19710261-0770]

large set-piece attack of the war for Canadians, the Battle of Valenciennes, was the result of a directive from Haig to General Horne to capture the city. This attack was to be carried out simultaneously with attacks by Third and Fourth Armies. The 51st Highland Division, part of 17th British Corps, began the attack with an assault on 28 October, but were unable to hold the ground gained.

The Canadian Corps took over employing the heaviest artillery bombardment in support of single brigade ever tried during the war. The 10th Brigade swept over Mont Houy, capturing stunned prisoners and reaching the edge of the city. Brigadier Andrew McNaughton, then serving as the senior Corps artillery officer, described the artillery program: "The barrage and bombardment had left scarcely a yard of ground untouched... the Canadian Corps had paid the price of victory ... in shells and not in life." Casualties were less than 400 with 80 killed in action. The next day the enemy abandoned Valenciennes.

The Second Canadian Division led the advance to Mons with orders to capture it if it could be done "without many casualties." Was the decision to maintain pressure based on the symbolism of Mons where the war, for the British Expeditionary Force, had begun more than four years before?

Currie was to say that "it would be befitting that the capture of Mons should close the fighting records of the Canadian Troops" but the reality was that all the leading divisions continued operations through to 1100 on 11 November. No Allied commander was willing to allow the enemy time to regroup and delay an Armistice including American commander John J. Pershing who was subjected to similar attacks after the war. On the 11th hour of the 11th day of the 11th month, the war ended.

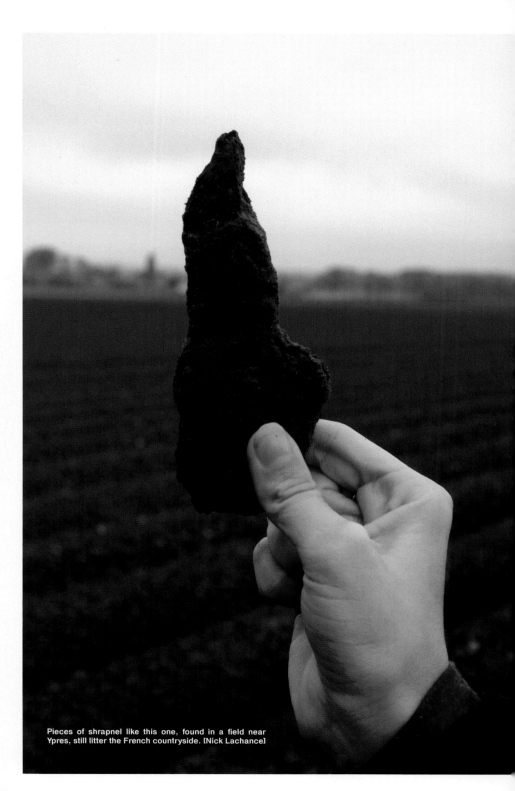

Pieces of shrapnel like this one, found in a field near Ypres, still litter the French countryside. [Nick Lachance]

NOTES ON BATTLEFIELD TOURING

YOUR TRIP WILL USUALLY begin at Charles de Gaulle airport. We have found that arriving a day ahead and staying in an airport hotel with a side trip into Paris and an early night allows us to overcome jetlag and start on the battlefield tour in good shape. The airport hotels located at Terminal 2, Ibis, Novotel and Sheraton, are the easiest to use but complementary transport to the less expensive and more varied hotels on the edge of the airport in Roissy-en-France is available from all terminals. If you do decide to travel into Paris, you can take the RER train from Terminal 2. Outside of rush hour a taxi may be a better option, especially if you are staying at a hotel in Roissy. An alternative, you may wish to consider travel to London, perhaps using the day flight from Toronto which arrives at Heathrow at 9:00pm local time. Use the next day to visit the much-enhanced Imperial War Museum and travel to Lille by the Eurostar. Car rental is easily arranged and all the major battlefields are close by.

We suggest you invest in a good GPS. Many car rental agencies will have them for rent but the price works out to be virtually the same as it is to buy. Many of the newer models are fully functional in Europe and North America. For your convenience we have placed in brackets beside each tour stop the exact address of each location (or its immediate vicinity). A number of GPS units have loaded attractions including a historical section that will sometimes have the exact area as well as a few sites you may want to visit. In Europe, where gas stations are not as plentiful as in North America, the GPS will also let you know where you can find fuel. Lodging and dining options are also available. Be sure to note the location and availability of all washrooms.

Although most of the historical monuments and cemeteries are well marked, the signs can also be easy to miss. They are usually slightly lower than signs in North America. Once you become familiar with their placement and appearance, however, you will notice them quite easily. Finally, the tours make for rather full days and have been designed in such a way as to include a number of sites.

Feel free to use this guidebook as a set of suggestions and depart from its recommendations as you see fit. Absolute must-see areas of the tour have been highlighted. In the end, the only way to cater to both the passing tourist and the military enthusiast was to make the guide as wide-ranging as possible.

TOUR

Touring the Ieper Salient

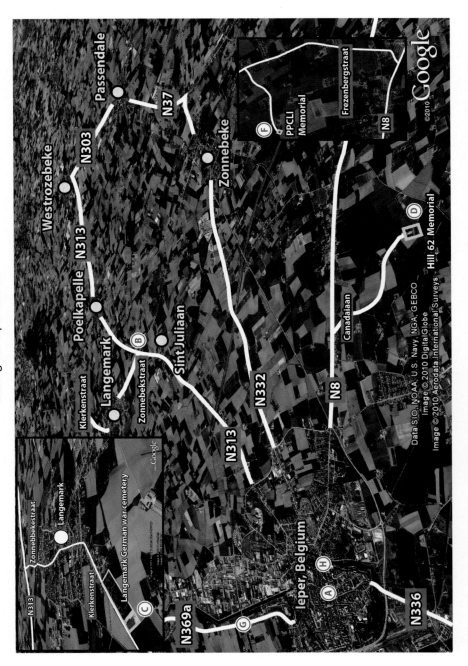

TOURING FLANDERS

FROM PARIS CHARLES DE Gaulle, follow the signs for "Autres Directions" then take the A1 autoroute north, "Direction Lille." This offers a trouble free drive away from the morning traffic in the Paris area. Your first stop might be L'Historial de la Première Guerre Mondiale. It is an outstanding museum and exhibition centre in Péronne, (A1 exit 13) follow the signs to L'Historial. There is free parking and local cafés for coffee or lunch. The museum provides an introduction to the military and cultural history of the Great War designed by leading experts in the field and features among other powerful exhibits the entire Der Krieg collection of drawings by Otto Dix, a German Expressionist painter who portrayed the agony of trench warfare in graphic images. There is also an excellent video on the Battle of the Somme that is well worth watching (www.historial.org).

From Péronne, Ieper (spelled Ypres during the war) is a two-hour drive from Péronne. We prefer to stay in the Novotel (GPS – Sint Jacobsstraat 15, 8900 Ieper, Belgium) which is a short walk from the Menin Gate and the Cloth Hall but there are a number of other hotels in the centre of town including the Albion and Ambrosia. The Ariane is a more expensive choice with its own excellent restaurant.

A Begin your tour in the Main Square and visit the "In Flanders Fields" Museum in the restored Cloth Hall in the centre of the town. The museum offers a multimedia introduction to the Great War which is cast as a plague-like tragedy for all nations—a common museum theme in context of European unity. The exhibits speak to the way in which soldiers and civilians experienced the war and an excellent diorama of the Ypres salient illustrates the destructive impact of the conflict for local people. As of 2014, each visitor receives a "personal" poppy bracelet with a microchip that automatically sets language and enables the visitor to discover four individual stories of those who lived or fought in the area. The bracelet may be kept as a souvenir.

B Next head northeast on the N313 towards the "Brooding Soldier" Memorial at Vancouver Corner in Sint Juliaan (GPS – Brugseweg 123, 8920 Langemark, Belgium). The French names in this part of Belgium have been changed to reflect the language of the Flemish majority so on most signs and maps St. Julien is Sint Juliaan. As you drive out of Ypres towards the northeast, you are following a route that would have been familiar to most Canadian and British troops serving in the salient as they moved to and from the frontlines. During the heavy fighting in 1914,

A student views an installation at the 'Historial de la Première Guerre Mondiale. [Nick Lachance]

1915, and 1917, this road was used to evacuate wounded from advanced dressing stations back to main dressing stations at Ypres and to the west.

As you pass to the east of Wieltje and cross under the A19, you are now entering the battlefield of April 1915. About 280 meters beyond to end of the town, you will cross the GHQ Line which in 1915 ran north to south through the buildings that now line the road. This was the last prepared line of defence in the Ypres salient. The line continued further to the north until it reached the "high ground" (the slight rise about a kilometre north of the modern road) of Mauser Ridge. On 22 April 1915, the German gas cloud drifted from the north towards Mauser Ridge, beginning to dissipate as it reached the crest which also marked the division between the French and Canadian lines. French troops streamed back through the fields north of the road into the rear

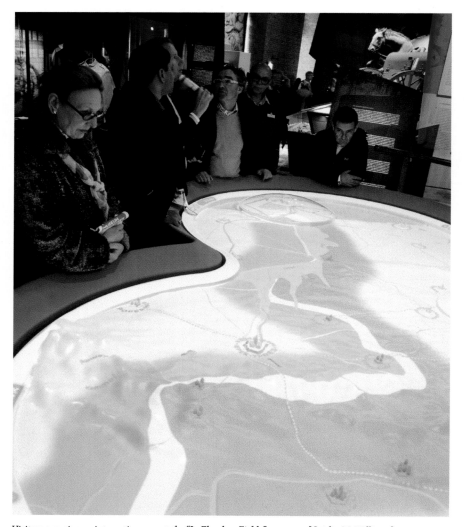

Visitors examine an interactive map at the "In Flanders Fields" museum. [Caitlin McWilliams]

The Brooding Soldier. [Nick Lachance]

areas of the Canadian lines and back towards Ypres. When you reach the junction of the N38 and N313, look out to the northwest where there is an enclosed Belgian farm about 250 meters away. In 1915, this was the approximate location of Mousetrap Farm which was Turner's 3rd Brigade Headquarters. Next you will reach Sint-Juliaan where, in the centre of the town, is a Commonwealth War Graves Cemetary near where one of the advanced Canadian dressing station was in 1915. During the battle, thousands of wounded soldiers were housed in the village as their comrades fought to hold the line to the west. About a kilometre to beyond the north end of the village is the Brooding Soldier memorial. The sculpture, designed by Canadian Frederick Clemesha, is surrounded by cedar trees that are trimmed in the shape of shells.

C Take time to visit the famous German military cemetery at nearby Langemarck. Head northwest on the Zonnebekestraat directly adjacent to the Brooding Soldier Monument. Follow the road through Langemarck-Poelkapelle where it changes to the Klerkenstraat. The cemetery is on the left (GPS – 8920 Langemarck-Poelkapelle, Belgium). Of note, the students decimated by British rifle fire during

Langemarck German Military Cemetery. [Nick Lachance]

Locations of The St. Eloi Craters

the German attack on Ypres in October 1914, are buried here (one of the large blocks to the far right when you enter). It is an event remembered in Germany as the Kindermord, or "Massacre of the Innocents." There is some debate but the bunkers in the cemetery are thought to have been constructed between Second Ypres (April 1915) and Third Ypres (June 1917) and were once part of the Hindenburg-Line that ran between Langemarck and Geluveld. They were restored for the official opening in 1932. There is a famous video clip of Adolf Hitler visiting this cemetery in 1940 on his tour through occupied Belgium and France. For those interested in war and memory, a trip 30 minutes north to the Vladslo German War Cemetery is strongly recommended (GPS – Houtlandstraat 3, 8600 Diksmuide, Belgium). Here the famed "The Grieving Parents" sculptures by Käthe Kollwitz watches over her youngest son Peter and 25,000 other German war dead.

D The next key location is the Canadian Memorial on Hill 62 (Mount Sorrel) at the end of a purpose-built road called the Canadalaan. (GPS – Canadalaan 26, 8902 Ypres, Belgium). From the Langemark Cemetery retrace your steps southeast to the N313. Continue south until you reach the N345 and turn left. Follow the N345 until you reach the N8 exit direction Meenseweg. Canadalaan, which is lined with maple trees, is less than a kilometre on your right. The Memorial is at the end of the road. On a clear day the strategic importance of Hill 62 is evident. The Canadian action to recapture the high ground denied the German Army a clear view into Ypres. To the northwest the Cloth Hall stands out on the horizon. The privately owned Sanctuary Wood Museum with its assorted collection of First World War ordnance, a network of trenches and shell craters to walk around, offers and a chance for coffee and a washroom break.

E The St. Eloi Craters are about a 10 minute drive from Hill 62. At the end of the Canadalaan, take a left on the N8 and at the roundabout, take the N37 south and west around Ieper. At the second on the N37 roundabout take the N336 south and you will eventually reach Sint Elooi. The original crater line ran through the ruined town in March 1916 when six new mines were exploded south of the town creating the confused battlefield which confronted Turner's division in early April. Continue on the N336 and immediately after the roundabout at the centre of the town veer to the left in the direction of the golf course. Just behind the large tower at the fork in the road, surrounded by trees, is Crater 4; Crater 5 is just a few more meters own the road. Directly behind you is Crater 3. All three craters are now ponds. If you are able to walk to the end of the private road which runs to the left of the tower you will be walking through the heart of the battlefield towards the positions of the 28th and 31st Battalions. The farm at the end of the road is built in the middle of the original crater line. These too are visible and filled with water on either side of house.

F Retrace your steps to the N8 heading towards Sanctuary Wood. About 10 minutes from Hill 62, in Frezenberg, lies the more obscure and less visited memorial to the Princess Patricia's Canadian Light Infantry (GPS – 38 Frezenberstraat, Zonnebeke, Vlaams Gewest, Belgium will take you to where you turn left at the Princess Patriciastraat). Pass by the turnoff onto the Canadalaan and continue on the N8. You will see signs for the monument that lead you onto Oude Kortrijkstraat on the left. Take your first left onto Frezenberstraat. Princess Patriciastraat will be on your left. The monument, on your right, is low to the ground and not well marked. The plaque reads "Here 8 May 1915 the "Originals" of Princess Patricia's Canadian Light Infantry commanded by their Founder Major A. Hamilton Gault, DSO, held firm and counted not the loss." As part of the BEF's 80th Brigade (nicknamed the "Stonewall Brigade" after its defence of Ypres), the Patricias suffered almost 400 casualties and were reduced to just four officers and 154 men at the end of the battle. Frezenberg is the graveyard of the original regiment and the Patricias first battle honour.

G Many Canadians make a point of visiting the Essex Farm Dressing Station and the British War Cemetery because of the association with Major John McCrae (GPS – John Mccraepad, 8900 Ieper, Belgium). Travel north along Frezenbergstraat to the A19 heading toward Veurne/Diksmuide/Poperinge. When the A19 ends, turn left at the N38 and follow the road across the Ieperlee Kanaal (formerly the Yser Canal) and take your first exit toward Diksmuiden. The Essex Farm Dressing Station and Cemetery are on your immediate left. Here overlooking the poppy-covered fields, McCrae composed In Flanders Fields. The

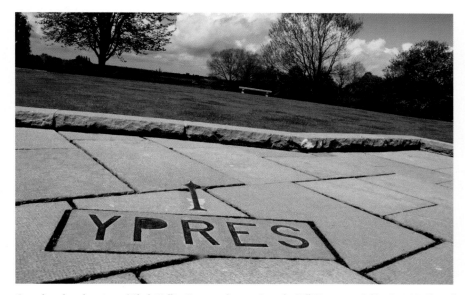

On a clear day, the spires of Cloth Hall in Ypres can be seen from the Hill 62 memorial. [Caitlin McWilliams]

The memorial to the Princess Patricias Canadian Light Infantry. [Matt Symes]

Dressing Stations are preserved directly adjacent to the graveyard. Be sure to visit the grave of Rifleman Valentine Joe Strudwick, one of the youngest Commonwealth soldier killed in the Great War at the age of 15. His grave is always adorned with a number of little wooden Remembrance Crosses and is easy to spot.

H Finally, return to Ieper's main square. The ceremony at the Menin Gate with the playing of the Last Post at 8:00pm is not to be missed. The Menin Gate was designed by Sir Reginald Blomfield and unveiled July 1927 by Field Marshal Lord Plumer. To the thousands of bereaved parents who had come for the inauguration or who were listening by radio back in Great Britain, Plumer offered the consolation the memorial was meant to convey: "He is not missing; he is here." Later generations would reject such phrases and their implication of willing sacrifice, but despite Wilfrid Owen and other war poets, official commemoration in 1927 evoked the idea of "Death So Noble." The Menin Gate bears the names of 54,896 soldiers, including 6,940 Canadians who died in the Ypres Salient before 16 August 1917. With the exception of the German occupation during the Second World War, the ceremony has carried on every night uninterrupted, by the fire brigade of Ypres, since 2 July 1928. If you would like to take part in the ceremony you can purchase a wreath from the tourist information centre in the Cloth Hall (You will exit into this area after you have finished visiting the In Flander's Field Museum) and speak to those in charge who can be seen organizing the ceremony around 7:30pm.

While based in Ieper you will no doubt wish to explore the battlefields of the Passchendaele offensive, described later in the tour section. Ieper is a fascinating place to visit. While you are there be sure to dine in the main square and visit the

View of the Menin Gate in Ieper, Belgium. [CWGC]

Menin Gate under construction. [CWGC]

British Grenadier bookshop near the Menin Gate. Steve Douglas, a Canadian who owns the store, is the man behind the Maple Leaf Legacy project, providing online photographs of every Canadian war grave (www.mapleleaflegacy.ca). For more information on other areas to tour in the Ypres Salient visit http://www.greatwar.co.uk and for tourist information, the Battlefields 1918 website. Click on "Ypres Salient" then "Ypres Tourism."

WALKING THE BATTLEFIELDS: KITCHENER'S WOOD (3 KILOMETRES)

1 Return from Sint-Juliaan towards Ypres on the N313. When you reach the sign indicating you are leaving the village, pull off just before you reach the line of trees beyond — there is a cobbled entrance to a field perfect for viewing the battlefield even on a rainy day. Standing at the field entrance, look to the northwest (307 degrees on a compass). About a kilometre away you will see a stand of trees in the middle of the field. There is a cluster of farm buildings just a bit further to the west. Those trees are all that remain of Kitchener's Wood. The woods used to stretch about 100 metres further towards the south west and east from those trees, and then a bit further north, they branched off several hundred meters to the north and east towards the small farm cluster in the middle distance (the one beyond the prominent windmill). We will use those trees and the farm complex to mark the approximate middle of the 1915 woods.

Looking to the west of the Kitchener's Wood farm complex, you'll see another cluster of trees and group of red roofed buildings (268 degrees on the compass). In 1915,

Walking the Battlefields: Kitchener's Wood

Sint Juliaan

Kitchener's Wood
(old boundaries)

Oblong Farm

Wijngaardstraat

Mouse Trap Farm

N 38

N 313

① ② ③ ④

N

that was Oblong Farm where the Germans sited several machineguns. Their frontline on the night of 22 April extended from behind Oblong Farm around the front of Kitchener's wood (so just to the rear of the modern farm) and then off to the northeast of St. Julian. The improvised Canadian frontline was close to the line formed by the N313. The approximate start line for the 10th and 16th Battalions on the night of 22 April 1915 was back where the high-voltage power-lines cross the N313.

2 After surveying the battlefield, return to your car and drive about 850 metres towards Ypres. Just past where the road divides into a boulevard, there is a turnoff to the right. Pull off and immediately park along the small road heading north (you'll notice the small red sign for the Kitchener's Wood Memorial facing traffic coming from Ypres). Just to your right, towards Seaforth Cemetery and the farm beyond, was where the 10th Battalion formed up, A Company on the right (near the cemetery), C on the left in two lines. B and D were about 30 yards behind. At 11:45 pm, the order was given to advance silently towards Kitchener's Wood. You can find the farm and cluster of trees that now mark the woods' old southern edge almost due north of where you are standing (352 degrees on a compass). You can now choose to walk along the edge of the battlefield, or drive, by following this road to the north.

3 As you move along the road, about 450 meters north of the N313, there is a slight widening of the pavement on the right at a field entrance surrounded by a clump of trees. Pause here standing in the gap in the trees. Looking out to the north and east, try to picture the men of the 10th Battalion running silently across the flat ground towards the woods in the dead of night. Now look to your left up the ever so slight rise to the cluster of trees and red roofed houses at what was Oblong Farm in 1915. Just beyond where you are standing, German machine guns firing in enfilade from that farm as well as straight on from the edge of the woods caught the 10th and 16th Battalions advancing in the open. Standing here in the middle of No-Man's-Land, it is easy to see why advances were so easily held up by a few machine guns in such open, flat country.

As you keep walking along the road, be sure to look along the edges of the farmers' fields. If weather and the state of the crops permits, you might also take the opportunity to look for shrapnel, bullets, and other battlefield relics in the dirt. Early spring is the best time of year, soon after the fields have been turned over, but we have always found 303 rounds, buttons, and shrapnel balls on our walks regardless of season.

4 About 600 metres further down the road, you will come to the Kitchener's Wood memorial standing at the corner of a small house. This modest monument was placed here in the late 1990s by the townspeople of Sint-Juliaan. The edge of the 1915 woods was about 200 metres to the east, near the modern edge of the small property. You can now return to the N313 by retracing your steps or by continuing on and taking the first road to the right which will connect back up with the road just east of Sint-Juliaan.

Touring the Ieper Salient

TOURING THE SOMME

WE HAVE ENJOYED STAYING in Amiens on several battlefield tours but we prefer to select a hotel in Arras for the two to four days devoted to the Somme, Vimy and the 1918 battles from Arras to Mons. If you are on a tight budget we recommend the Ibis Centre in the heart of the city. The Mercure Atria and Holiday Inn Express at the railway station plaza offer better, larger rooms. The Mercure has a pleasant restaurant with good food. Les Trois Luppars in the Grand Place offers a more traditional location and we have enjoyed staying here. The liveliest restaurant-café scene is in the Place des Héros, but if you are after better cuisine consider the Faisanderie or Rapière in the Grand Place. One disadvantage to staying in Arras is missing the cathedral in Amiens which is one of the glories of the Western world. Listed as a UNESCO World Heritage Site, this 13th century marvel is the largest cathedral in France. There are a number of plaques commemorating Canadian regiments and battles but the building speaks for itself. Amiens is a short drive west of Pozières. The cathedral is visible from the edge of the town and is well marked.

Mary Riter Hamilton, "The Sadness of the Somme." [LAC 1988-180-19]

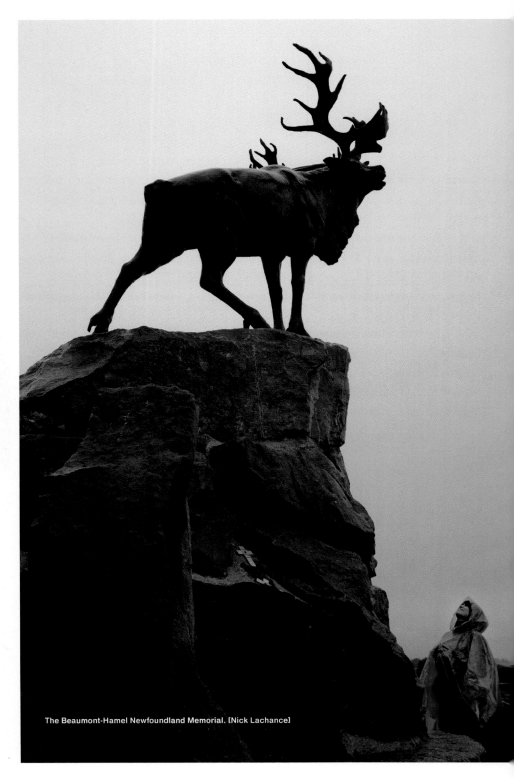

The Beaumont-Hamel Newfoundland Memorial. [Nick Lachance]

A For Canadians, a visit to the Somme must begin at the Newfoundland Memorial Park at Beaumont-Hamel (GPS – 80300 D73, Auchonvillers, France). From Arras, take the D917 south to the D929 which bypasses Baupaume, continue west on the D929 to Pozières then right at the Canadian sign to Beaumont-Hamel. You will pass by Thiepval and the Ulster Tower before reaching the well-marked park where Canadian university students will greet you and offer a guided tour or a detailed map for a self-guided walk. Be sure to walk up to the top of the monument for a good view over the battlefield. As you walk through No-Man's-Land to the cemetery, you will come across the Danger Tree encased in cement. Soldiers used this tree to guide themselves back to their own positions after night raids. The Germans, who knew this, used this lone mark to range their guns, hence the nickname "Danger Tree." In Y Ravine Cemetery look for the Caribou Regimental Insignia of the Newfoundland Regiment. As the path turns slightly left you will see Y Ravine – The German front line. There is also a large monument to the 51st Scottish Highlanders on the grounds overlooking Y Ravine and the scene of their successful assault on the German defences 13 November 1916. Look across the farmer's field and you will see a clump of trees in the distance. Note how their tops are level with the farming ground. These are the trees that have grown in Hawthorn Crater (if you continue northwest along the D73 and take the first right down a farmer's road to get to the site as well as Hawthorn Ridge Cemetery No. 1).

B The next major action of the Canadian Corps on the Somme is Courcelette but there are some worthwhile stops along the way. The Ulster Tower Memorial commemorates the 36th Ulster Division (GPS – 80300 D73, Thiepval, France). Continue back along the D73 toward Pozières and you cannot miss the tower on your left. The monument is nearly an identical replica of Helen's Tower in Bangor, County Down, Northern Ireland which stood on the estate where many of the men of the Ulster Division trained before heading to France. An audio/visual presentation explains the initial success of the Ulster Division on 1 July 1916 and illustrates their isolation before a forced withdrawal. There is a small café, bookstore, and washrooms. Please note, it is closed on Sundays and Mondays.

C Continuing toward Pozières on the D73, the Thiepval Memorial is the British "Vimy" (GPS – Rue de L'Ancre, 80300 Thiepval, France). Standing 45 metres high with the names of 73,367 British soldiers who have no known grave listed on the pillars, Thiepval is the largest British War Memorial in the world. More than 90 percent of the names listed died between July and November 1916. At the foot of the memorial 300 British and 300 French soldiers, are buried together to commemorate the joint nature of the 1916 offensive. In 2004 an impressive interpretation centre run by the British Legion opened.

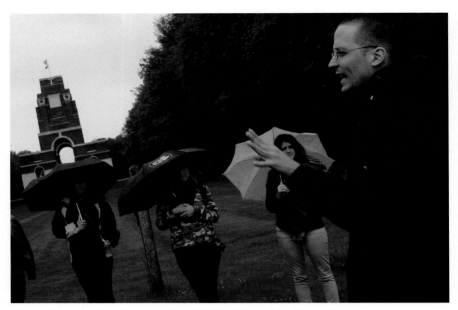

Students discuss the 1916 offensive in front of the Thiepval Memorial. [Nick Lachance]

D As you make your way to the Courcelette battlefields along the D73 it is worth a brief stop at Mouquet Farm (GPS – la Ferme du Mouquet, 8300, Ovilliers-la-Boisselle, France). Over the course of August and early September the Australians managed to reach the farm three times but were forced back each time as German artillery rained down on them from the three sides of the salient.

E For those interested in the First Australian Division Monument in Pozières and the viewing platform looking over the battlefield take a right on Rue de L'Église just before the D929 (GPS – 333 Rue de L'Église, 8300 Pozières, France). As the road veers toward the D929 the monument will be on your right. The viewing platform that clearly illustrates the sweeping views the Germans held over the advancing Allied troops is across the road.

F To visit the Courcelette battlefields, head east on the D929. On the edge of Pozières you will find a memorial to the men of the tank Corps (GPS – 977 Route de Baupaume, 8300 Contalmaison, France). The monument commemorates the first use of the 'landships' in battle with scale models of the tanks used here in 1916. Across the road, the Windmill Memorial to the First Australian Division provides a good vantage point to survey the ground over which the Canadians fought in the fall of 1916. Directly ahead on the left side of the highway is the "Sugar Factory," rebuilt after the war on the original site. The steeple of the church in Courcelette is visible as is the rising ground beyond that gave the Germans an overview of the preparations for the advance to Courcelette.

G The Canadian Memorial for the 1916 Somme battles is about 800 metres further northeast on the D929 before the village of Courcelette (GPS – N Route Nationale, 8300 Martinpuich, France will take you to the Sugar Factory from which you cannot miss the Canadian Memorial). Parking is available across the highway.

H The village of Courcelette was completely destroyed in 1916 but has been largely rebuilt on the original footprint. Continue beyond the village to the Courcelette British cemetery (GPS – 42 Rue du Grand Chemin, 8300 Courcelette France). From the monument take a left onto the D107. Take your second left onto Rue du Chapitre which will turn into Gr. Grand Rue and guide directly to the cemetery. There are 1,970 Commonwealth soldiers buried here including 16-year-old Private George Ritchie from the Royal Canadian Dragoons and 17-year-old John Robertson from the 43rd Battalion Canadian Infantry, Manitoba Regiment. If you walk along the edges of the farm track continuing beyond the cemetery with a keen eye you will still find shell casings, shrapnel, and other bits of ordnance from the war. The German trench line the Canadians called "Regina" crossed the road just beyond the cemetery.

I Regina Trench Cemetery, located on the site of the actual German earthworks, is north of the village in the middle of farmland and is well marked. Retrace your steps back to Courcelette about 700 metres and take a left and continue northwest for about 1.5 kilometres. The original cemetery, where the graves are closer, was put together in the winter of 1916-1917. There are now more than 2,000 Commonwealth soldiers buried here including American pilot Lieutenant Ervin Shaw. Shaw's gravestone is directly beside his observer, Sergeant Thomas Smith, in what is a common practice to bury aircrew in graves that virtually touch each other.

A view from Regina Trench looking towards Desire Trench. [Nick Lachance]

J You will want to visit Adanac Cemetery (Canada spelled backwards) on the D107 between Courcelette and Miraumont (GPS – D107, 8300 Courcelette, France. This point will take you to the edge of Courcelette on the D107 headed toward the cemetery 1.3 kilometres north). Adanac cemetery is the final resting place of 1,072 Canadians among the 3,186 men buried here. Among the Canadians, Private (Piper) James Richardson is buried here. The 20-year-old from Chilliwack B.C. was awarded the Victoria Cross for playing his company over the top. As the company approached Regina Trench they came under intense fire and Piper Richardson "strode up and down outside the wire, playing his pipes with the greatest coolness…" His comrades "rushed the wire with such fury and determination that the obstacle was overcome and the position captured." Losses among the assault battalions were so heavy that the captured sections of Regina Trench could not be held. Richardson survived the battle but later died in an attempt to retrieve his pipes which he had laid down while helping a wounded soldier in no-man's-land. His pipes, which sat in a Scottish school unidentified for almost a century, were repatriated in 2006.

The 1916 battlefields of the Somme include some of the most visited sites in Northern France. Quite apart from regular tourists and tour busses, there will be numerous student tour groups shepherded by anxious teachers. Patience may be required. You may also want to visit The Somme Trench Museum (Musée des Abris - Somme 1916) in Albert, which focuses on the July 1916 offensive and the realities of trench warfare (http://www.somme-trench-museum.co.uk). A series of dioramas are presented in tunnels once used to shelter the inhabitants. The museum is located beside the Basilica in the centre of Albert (GPS – Rue Anicet Godin, 80300 Albert, France).

There are a few other locations not directly involving the Canadians that are worth seeing if you have the time. The South African Museum and National Memorial at Longueval was built in the Apartheid era as part of a public relations campaign. The features of the original are intact though the message has changed. The attached museum tells the story of the battle for Delville Wood (GPS – Route de Ginchy, 8360 Longueval, France). For those with a Welsh background the unique Red Dragon Memorial in commemoration of the 38th (Welsh) Division attacks on Mametz Wood is a must see. (GPS – Bois Santin, 8300 Bazentin, France. If you are coming from Pozières you will pass a Commonwealth cemetery on your right and if you are coming from Mametz the monument will be on your right). The Welsh Division suffered 4,000 casualties between 7 and 12 July 1916 but were ultimately successful in clearing the forested area. The famous poet Siegfried Sassoon fought in the engagement and modernist novelist David Jones wrote about the attack in his work "In Parenthesis." For information on other areas to see on the Somme battlefield visit: www.somme-battlefields.com.

WALKING THE BATTLEFIELDS:
DESIRE TRENCH (3 KILOMETRES)

The attack on Desire Trench was the final phase in the long Somme battle on 18 November 1916. That morning, the 11th Canadian Infantry Brigade and elements of the 12th Brigade advanced with British units on either flank towards the villages of Grandcourt and Miraumont. The Canadians managed to capture the Desire Trench system but the units on their flanks were less successful. Although relatively unknown, the battlefield today is almost perfectly preserved which makes it an exciting place to take a walk.

1 Start at Regina Trench Cemetery. Regina Trench, which was captured a few days before the attack, was also the starting point for the assault. The original trench line ran through the modern cemetery approaching almost straight from the west and then turning northeast as shown on the map. The 38th Canadian Infantry Battalion from Ottawa held a position just to the east and rear of the cemetery along the current field boundary. On 18 November it was to advance due north towards the German lines.

2 If you stand at the northern corner of the cemetery, about 650 metres away (compass heading 2.5 degrees) was a switch in the German front line. Where you now see a stand of trees in the valley below, the German line ran southwest to northeast following a natural sunken valley and the roll of the ground. This was Desire Trench which was connected to Grandcourt Trench, about 600 metres further north, via another sunken road. The German defences included a cluster of machine-gun nests at this junction (marked 4 on your map) and smaller groups of guns about 250 metres to the east and west.

3 The Battalion went over the top following a rolling barrage, but soon lost it crossing the pockmarked ground. If you are careful to work your way along the edge of the field rows or through the crop lines, you can easily walk the same line of advance more or less towards the German lines to the north. An old road and field boundary marked 3 on your map is often useful for this purpose but you may also choose to go direct across country. If conditions do not permit you to do this without damaging crops, you can follow the other road to the left of Regina trench for about 130 metres to the northwest, making a fifty metre jog to the left, and then continuing on to the right about 420 meters to the northwest. There a small road turns off to the right, take it 620 metre to the northeast and when you reach the sharp turn to the north. Keep your eyes out in the fields for small grey metal pebbles: the balls from the many shrapnel shells fired here throughout the war.

4 Whether you cross the field or take the road, when you come to the bottom of the valley, you will find a sunken, tree-lined road running to the north.

Walking the Battlefields: Desire Trench

Machine-gunners firing from the lip of the natural depression in the ground caught the 38th Battalion out in the open as they advanced from Regina Trench, inflicting heavy casualties. Take a minute to look back towards the cemetery and observe their lines of sight. Thain Wendall MacDowell, a Captain who would later win the Victoria Cross at Vimy Ridge, won the Distinguished Conduct Medal right here by knocking out several machineguns with bombs and German rifles seized from the dead. He then led several teams of bombers up the sunken road and into Grandcourt Trench beyond.

5 Follow the sunken road he took about 600 metres to the north. During the war, this same route would have been used by the Germans to ferry rations, ammunition, and men to Desire Trench and the remnants of their defences including concrete emplacements, metal fragments, and barbed wire are still visible in the underbrush. Eventually you will reach another junction with an option to go right or veer to the left. Goa as far as you can to the right, a couple dozen metres. These are the remains of Grandcourt Trench which also followed an old sunken road and natural depressions in the ground. When you consider how far you have come, contemplate that Macdowell and his men made the same trip in a few minutes under heavy fire. The 38th and 78th Battalions eventually established posts in Grandcourt trench that later had to be withdraw because they were too far beyond the new frontline at Desire Trench. This illustrates a key problem during the war: advances, even when successful, often outstripped both artillery support and logistics.

You can now return to Regina Trench by retracing your steps or explore the remains of the valley. Relics and signs of war are everywhere, but be careful not to get lost in the maze of paths and sunken roads many of which follow old trench lines. You can also work your way to the west to the other road which will take you back towards Coucellete to the south, affording a different view of the battlefield. This can be a long walk though unless you are able to cut across the field towards Regina Trench.

Touring Vimy

TOURING VIMY

A BEGIN YOUR STUDY OF Vimy at Notre-Dame de Lorette (GPS – Colline de Notre-Dame de Lorette, 62153 Ablain-Saint-Nazaire, France). From Arras head north on the D937 to Souchez and turn left on the D57. Turn right at the Rue de la Blanc Voie and veer left at the fork continuing on the same road up the hill to the cemetery. It is well marked. This is the site of the French national cemetery and memorial for the battles of 1914-1915 and is well worth visiting in its own right. Over 45,000 French soldiers are buried in this cemetery. The crypt near the basilica contains the tombs of unknown French soldiers from many First World War battles. At the far end of the cemetery (to your left from the main gates) you will find the Jewish and Muslim graves.

B To understand the battles for Vimy Ridge walk to the observation areas that overlook the battlefield. The gently sloping western side of the Vimy escarpment is laid out before you. The twin pylons of the memorial are visible on clear days 4 kilometres away and you can gain some idea of the scale of the Corps battle that was fought here. The significance of the French Army's operations in the spring and fall of

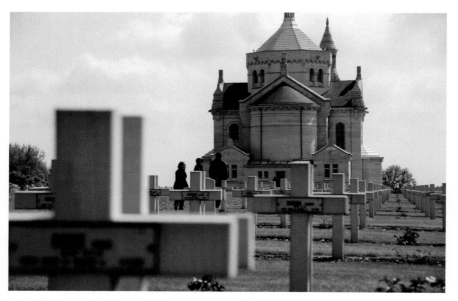

The basillica at Notre-Dame de Lorette. [Caitlin McWilliams]

BURES

MORT POUR LA FRANCE

Cross grave markers at Notre-Dame de Lorette.
[Caitlin McWilliams]

1915 when the Tenth Army reached but could not hold Vimy Ridge will quickly be apparent. Without Allied control of the Lorette Spur and the withdrawal of the German defensive positions onto the ridge it is unlikely that any attack would have succeeded.

Orient yourself by identifying the Vimy Memorial at Point 145 and the jagged towers at Mont St. Eloi to the south. The map on p.54 highlights the sectors through which the four Canadian divisions attacked as well as the artillery positions on the Lorette Ridge and in the valley below. Each of these sectors can be explored if you have time but most visitors to Vimy need the better part of a day to visit the memorial, the tunnels and the interpretation centre.

C On your way to Vimy, you should go by way of the small church in Ablain St. Nazaire (GPS – 1 Blanche Voie Street, 62153 Ablain-Saint-Nazaire, France). Go west on the D58E3 and then left onto the steep Rue de la Blanche Voie. In May 1915, French troops stormed up this nearly vertical face of the Lorette Spur in heavy fighting. At the bottom of the hill, you will enter the village of Ablain St. Nazaire; stay on the Rue de la Blanche Voie as it veers to the right. On your left are the ruins of a 15th century church, destroyed during the fighting in the spring of 1915. Pay attention to signage, but if it is safe to do so, you can enter the ruins of the church to look for graffiti left by Canadian and British soldiers. In the spring of 1917, and again in May 1940, artillery units were stationed here and men carved their names, units, and hometowns into the walls. Be mindful of nettles and your footing.

Continue on to Vimy via Cabaret Rouge War Cemetery (GPS – 1 Rue Carnot 62153 Souchez, France). Continue on the Rue de la Blanche Voie and turn left at the junction with the D57. You are now driving along routes used in 1917 to ferry

The muslim section of the cemetery at Notre-Dame de Lorette. [Caitlin McWilliams]

ammunition and supplies up from the Canadian Corps' rear areas to the front. In Souchez, turn right onto the D937. The cemetery is about 600 metres from the edge of the town on your right. It is from this cemetery in 2000 that the remains of an unidentified Canadian soldier were exhumed and laid to rest within the Tomb of the Unknown Soldier in front of the War Memorial in Ottawa. Oliver and Wilfred Chenier, brothers from Buckingham, Quebec, who died on the first day of the Battle of Vimy Ridge are also buried here.

D You should start your tour of Vimy at the visitation centre taking time to explore the replica trenches and the underground tunnels (GPS – Route des Canadiens 62580 Thélus, France). From Cabaret Rouge Cemetery continue south on the D937 and turn left on Rue du 11 Novembers. Veer left on Rue du Carlin and another left on the D55. Cross the A26 and it turns into Route des Canadiens where the interpretation center is. The rebuilt trenches are interesting to visit, although they are not exactly a realistic depiction of what the position would have looked like. The publicly accessible tunnels are fascinating albeit heavily sanitized. There are kilometres of tunnels honeycombing the site, but these are closed to the public because of safety concerns. If you are with a small group you can sign up on the day but if you are with a large group (more than 6) you will need a reservation to visit the tunnels. To book a tour go to the Veterans Affairs Canada website and click on the links or email vimy_memorial@vac-acc.gc.ca. The phone number in France is 33 321 58 5834. From Canada, dial 011 before the 33. It is not possible to purchase lunch in the park so remember to bring sandwiches which you will only be allowed to eat in the parking lot where there are a few picnic tables. The Vimy Foundation is raising funds to build a new interpretation centre here.

Sheep graze in shell craters near Vimy Ridge. [Nick Lachance]

"Mother Canada" overlooks the Lens-Douai plain. [Caitlin McWilliams]

E Next drive to the parking lot by the memorial. Before you visit the monument take a moment to look across the road from the upper parking lot at the Moroccan Division Memorial. It commemorates the members of the French Moroccan Division who fought their way to this point in 1915.

F As you walk toward the Vimy Memorial, designed by Walter Allward, you cannot help but be impressed by its sheer size and beauty. Jonathan Vance, who wrote the award-winning study of the Canadian memory of the Great War Death So Noble, called Vimy "Canada's primary altar to the fallen of war." At the time Arthur Currie worried that the monument would overshadow other, greater, Canadian achievements even if he conceded that "there it was that the Canadian Corps first fought as a unit and, as its components were drawn from all parts of the country, Vimy may be considered as the first appearance of our young nation at war." That Point 145 is such a striking physical landscape played just as important a role in deciding the location for Allward's design.

The Twin columns of the Vimy Memorial represent France and Canada, partners in arms. As you approach the monument the male and female sculptures on the right and left represent Mourning Parents. The Statues at the top of the columns represent Truth and Knowledge. As you wrap about the monument you see Mother Canada mourning her dead. In the middle of the two pillars sits the Spirit of Sacrifice and the Passing of the Torch. As you descend the stair case and look back at the monument from the grass you see what represents an impenetrable Wall of Defence. On the southern side you have the Breaking of the Swords and on the northern edge the Sympathy of the Canadians for the Helpless. In the middle

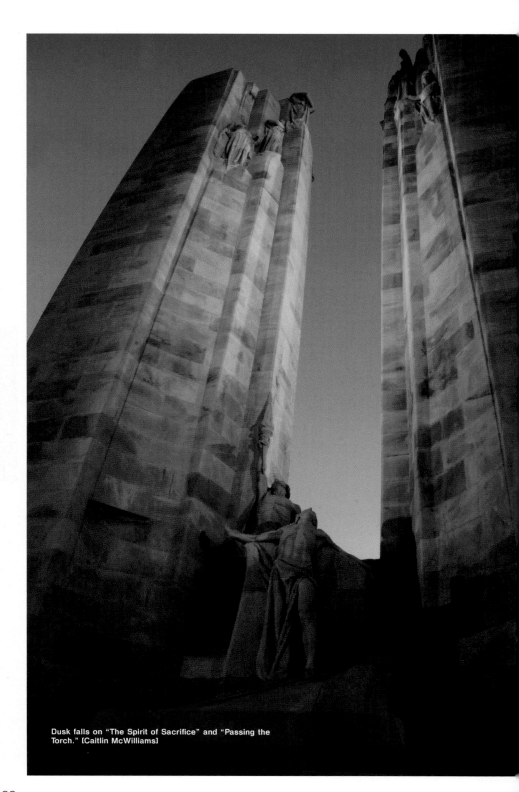

Dusk falls on "The Spirit of Sacrifice" and "Passing the Torch." [Caitlin McWilliams]

sits the Stone Sarcophagus representing Canada's killed soldiers. Though there is a deeply religious feel to the Vimy Memorial, the direct references are subtle. The wall and pillars represented the top of a cross and the sunlight on the monument was meant to give the effect of a cathedral.

The 11,285 names of missing Canadians with no known grave around the base of the Vimy Memorial were not part of the original design. The addition of the names of the missing was one of several alterations to the original design of the monument. This change transformed Vimy into hallowed ground, an empty tomb and therefore a place of pilgrimage. Allward also agreed to modify his "Breaking the Sword" sculpture which originally included a German helmet crushed under the foot of one of the figures. This was done to avoid "militaristic imagery."

The memorial was unveiled in 1936 with thousands of Canadian Veterans and their families present for the Vimy pilgrimage. The pilgrimage like the memorial was full of ambiguities. Was it a celebration of the achievement of the Canadian Corps or a ceremony mourning the missing? Did the presence of King Edward VIII suggest an imperial event solidifying Canada's relationship with Britain or a statement about an independent Canadian nation? Was the monument to be seen as a remonstrance against war or a warning to the enemies of democracy that Canada would again play its part in defending Britain and France against German aggression? It was all these things and more.

Of the more than 65,000 Canadians killed in the Great War, 7,000 are buried in 30 cemeteries within a 20 kilometre radius of the Vimy Memorial. It would be virtually impossible to visit every Canadian grave, but if you have time make your way to La Chaudière Military Cemetery (GPS - 3-5 Route Nationale, 62580 Vimy, France). The burial ground, which was originally called Vimy Canadian Cemetery No. 1, is shaped like an artillery shell. Among the 638 Canadian soldiers buried here is Victoria Cross recipient Private John George Pattison, 50th Canadian Infantry, (Alberta Regiment).

On your way back to Arras you might consider visiting one of the three divisional memorials, placed shortly after the battle to honour the part played by the Canadian Corps in taking and holding Vimy Ridge. The easiest to find is the monument to the Second Division on the western edge of Thélus at the junction of the D49 and the N17 (GPS – 32 Rue des Artilleurs Canadiens, Thélus, France).

A tour of the area immediately east and north of Arras is not really recommended until the proposed Hill 70 monument is built. Urbanization, traffic and the absence of memorials or viewing points make for a difficult day and little to see. If you are determined to see Hill 70 and Lens consult Norm Christie's guidebook Other Canadian Battlefields of the Great War in his "For King and Empire" series. For current information search for "Arras Tourism-Battlefields." The official site has hotel links and other tourist information.

Members of the 2013 War and Memory tour meet in front of "The Wall of Defence." [Nick Lachance]

You might wish to visit the Arras Memorial and Flying Services Memorial located two kilometres west of the railway station on Blvd. Charles de Gaulle. Follow signs for La Citadelle, in the Faubourg-d'Amiens Commonwealth Cemetery. The Arras Memorial commemorates the 34,718 British, New Zealand and South African troops who died in the Arras sector and who have no known graves. The Flying Services Memorial commemorates the airmen who died in Northern France including the 207 fatalities in April 1917. There are 153 Canadians buried in the cemetery. Make time for the underground museum Carrière Wellington which is open every day from 10:00am-12:30pm and 1:30-6:00pm. (http://www.carriere-wellington.com). It provides real insight into the lives of soldiers and civilians. The website offers links to hotels, restaurants, and other activities in the Arras region.

WALKING THE BATTLEFIELDS:
3RD DIVISION AT VIMY RIDGE (4.5 KILOMETRES)

The 3rd Division's advance on 9 April was led by the 7th (left) and 8th (right) Canadian Infantry Brigades. You will be following the path of the 1st Canadian Mounted Rifles (CMRs) which were part of the 8th Brigade. The 1st CMRs' objectives included the German front lines 200 metres from their start line, the intermediate position (Zwichen-Stellung) 600 metres further to the east, and a sunken road running through the edge of La Folie woods a further kilometre beyond. For an overview of the 3rd Division attack, see the essay by Geoffrey Hayes in *Vimy Ridge: A Canadian Reassessment.*

1 Begin your walk at the eastern edge of Neuville Saint-Vaast where the Rue de Vimy crosses over the Autoroute des Anglais (GPS – 6-14 Rue de Vimy, 62580 Neuville-Saint-Vaast, France). You can get there from the Vimy Interpretation Centre by taking the D55 south into Neuville Saint-Vaast and about 100 metres beyond the sign indicating you are entering the town, veer to the left onto the Rue des Meuiers. At the next stop sign, go left onto the Rue de Vimy and park just before you reach the bridge over the autoroute. You are now standing about 500 metres behind the CMRs frontline. On 8 April D Company held the foremost trenches while C, B, and A Companies were billeted just behind were you are standing in the ruins of Neuville Saint-Vaast. At about 2:00 am on 9 April, these three companies began moving up to new jumping off positions that had been prepared just behind those taken over by D Company. To follow their route, cross the bridge over the AutoRoute and walk down the dirt road to where it meets another road coming in from the southeast (about 300 metres).

2/3/4 The road running off to the south provides an approximate indication of what would have been considered the start of the frontline area on 9 April (you can also walk along this road for about 400 metres to Lichfield Crater cemetery which is a fascinating example of a crater burial site). The CMRs jumping off positions were another 125-50 metres further to the east, down the dirt road leading into the woods, just past where a small track breaks off to the north.

As you walk through the woods, you can see the pockmarked ground preserved by the modern forest. Old trench lines are also visible through the trees, marked by zig-zag depressions in the ground. As you cross the old Canadian frontline, approximately at the place marked Point 3, where the track breaks off to the north, you are entering No-Man's-Land. At 5:30 am on 9 April, D company advance from near this point behind a rolling barrage onto the German frontlines. Even on 9 April, the German trenches were largely unrecognizable thanks to an effective preparatory barrage. Walking along the dirt road, about 320 metres further on, you will cross a noticeable depression running north south at about Point 4. This was the approximate position of the German frontline trench. The 1st CMRs reported reaching this point just as the Germans opened up with their own counter-barrage as flares "of all colours" could be seen rising from the Zwichen-Stellung. Depending on the season, it's still possible to see the remnants of the defensive line here.

5 Keep walking about 500 metres further down the road in an east-northeast direction. When you reach the main paved road (Route des Canadiens), you should detour north to the 3rd Division monument, marked Point 5 on your map. To do so, follow the paved road north for 200 metres, taking the first path to the right along the northern side of the large field to the east. In 1917, this was La Folie

Walking the Battlefields: 3rd Division at Vimy Ridge

Farm, marked Point 5b. The 3rd Division monument is in the middle of the field along the line of advance of the 4th and 2nd CMRs. It is built on the approximate position of the Geman Zwichen-Stellung. The old trench line, marked Point 5a on your map, can sometimes be seen in the middle of the field, depending on the state of the vegetation, running to the south away from the monument along where the taller bushes are growing in the midst of the shorter grasses. The soil at Vimy is naturally filled with chalk so when the trenches were excavated and later filled in, the vegetation that grows in the old trench lines is slightly different from the native grasses. Keep your eyes out for the zig-zag of nettles and brush in fallow fields throughout the region.

6/7/8 When you are done at the monument, return to where the dirt road you took through the woods met the Rue des Canadiens. You are now standing at the approximate location of the German intermediate position. On 9 April, C, B, and A companies leap-frogged D Company, reaching the Zwichen-Stellung soon after. The Battalion war diary records:

Very little opposition was encountered from this trench, which was supposed to be the enemy's strong line. The barrage was followed by the troops step by step until the trench was finally reached. As on the front line, the wire along Zwichen Stellung had been completely cut by our artillery, and the trench itself had been knocked to pieces, and practically all the dugouts smashed in.

The Zwichen-Stellung crossed the modern Rue des Canadiens just past where it meets the dirt road and turns north, about at Point 6; the German position of bunkers, trenches, and machinegun emplacements extended a further 100 metres beyond. Follow the walking trail along the road at Point 7 towards the 1st CMRs' final objective a further kilometre and a half away. This was the portion of the advance given to B and A Companies and although they encountered only sporadic resistance, enemy shelling and fatigue ensured that by the time they reached their final goal, only about 50 or 60 men were available to consolidate the line. Fortunately, little resistance was encountered. It is possible to continue following the Canadian advance all the way to the edge of town of Le Petite Vimy, to Point 8, but the trails through the woods beyond where the Rue des Canadiens turns to the south are a honeycomb of dead-ends and sharp turns. It is inadvisable to continue on without a reliable GPS. If you do not have a GPS, we advise you to retrace your steps.

Touring Passschendaele

TOURING PASSCHENDAELE

IT IS QUITE IMPOSSIBLE to obtain any sense of what the area looked like in 1917. The village (now spelled Passendale) has been completely rebuilt, not restored, and though the farm land still yields shells and other ordnance fragments from the war, the drainage has been restored and the landscape appears unscarred. When the Canadians entered the battle, the British-Australian frontline included the hamlet of Gravenstafel.

A For those looking for a general overview of the battle begin your day at the "Passchendaele Memorial Museum" in Zonnebeke (GPS – Ieperstraat 5, B-8980 Zonnebeke). From Ieper take the N37 north to Zonnebeke and turn right on Berten Pilstraat where the museum is well marked. The Passchendaele Memorial Museum, located on the grounds of a rebuilt Chateau, has numerous artifacts and audio/visual presentations on the 1917 battle though the Canadian contribution is lumped in with the British forces. The trenches in the basement that greet visitors as they leave give an eerie claustrophobic feel that allows you to experience a bit of what

Mary Riter Hamilton, "Canadian Monument Near Passchendaele," which features the monument to the 85th (Nova Scotia) Battalion. [LAC 1988-180-114].

The Canadian Memorial at Passchendaele. [Matt Symes]

it must have been like during the Great War. There is an excellent restaurant on the grounds. Consult the website for hours and events (http://www.passchendaele.be).

B The Canadian Memorial for the battle is located west of the village on the Canadalaan (GPS – Route 66 bvba Canadalaan 39, near 8980 Passendale, Belgium). Return to the N37/N332 heading north and turn left on the N303 north toward the centre of Passendale. Take a moment and stop at the Church in the centre of Passendale that has striking stained glass windows dedicated to the British 66th Division. Two impressive bronze plaques describing the various battles in the salient and providing information on the battle for Passchendaele are located in the square beside the church.

C Continue along Canadalaan which will take you directly to the Canadian Memorial. The inscription reads "The Canadian Corps in Oct-Nov 1917 advanced across this valley, then a treacherous morass – captured and held Passchendaele Ridge." It is possible to look back to the spires of Ypres from the memorial, a sharp reminder of just how limited the advance was.

Among those who died in the battle to seize the ridge was Major Talbot Mercer Papineau who had publicly debated the meaning of the war and Canada's national identity with his cousin, the French Canadian nationalist Henri Bourassa. In an open letter to Bourassa, who was opposed to further Canadian participation in the war, Papineau declared that "French and English Canadians are fighting and dying side by side…Is their sacrifice to go for nothing or will it not cement a foundation for a true Canadian nation,…independent in thought, independent in action, independent even in its political organization – but in spirit united for high international and humane purposes to the two Motherlands of England and France?" Later in the letter he argued that "As a [French] minority in a great English-speaking continent,... we must rather seek to find points of contact and of common interest than points of friction and separation." Words that also needed to be addressed to English-speaking Canadians. Bourassa mocked Papineau for having written to him in English - an indication of his limited connection with French Canada. Despite having secured a position behind the lines working for Canadian War Records Office, Major Papineau felt obligated to rejoin his battalion, the Princess Patricia's Canadian Light Infantry, in 1917. On October 30, moments before going over the top, Papineau's uttered his final recorded words to Major Hugh Wilderspin: "You know, Hughie, this is suicide." As you move to the 85th (Nova Scotia Highlanders) Battalion Memorial you will pass by Papineau's wartime makeshift grave that was lost to the carnage of Passchendaele.

D The 85th (Nova Scotia) Battalion Monument is located down a grass track on the south edge of the village off the N303/N37 toward Tyne-Cot (GPS – Passendalestraat 80, 8980 Passendale, Belgium). The location, on the left hand side, is not well marked and easily missed. The monument was originally raised in 1919 by the regiment before returning home. It was erected on the site of the battalion's headquarters during the battle. It commemorates the 85th Battalion's costliest action of the war where the "Neverfails" as they became known, lost 148 men. A new monument, a replica of the original but made of Nova Scotia granite, was rededicated in 2001.

E End your visit at Tyne Cot Cemetery, the largest Commonwealth war cemetery in the world and the only one in which the Cross of Sacrifice is located on top of a German pill-box (GPS – Tynecotstraat 29, 8980 Zonnebeke, Belgium). Continue south on the N303/N37 and turn right on Tynecotstraat. The visitation

A student walks between headstones at Tyne Cot. [Nick Lachance]

Headstones undergo routine maintenance at Tyne Cot Cemetery. [Caitlin McWilliams]

center and the parking lot is well-marked on your right. Looking to the northeast, you can survey the approaches to the ridge. The Visitor Centre opened in 2007 serves to individualize the more than 200,000 Commonwealth casualties suffered at Passchendaele. The northeast boundary of the cemetery features the memorial to the missing with 34,887 names of British and New Zealand men who were killed after 16 August 1917 with no known grave. It was at Tyne Cot cemetery, near the end of his of his pilgrimage, that King George V said in a speech, "I have many times asked myself whether there can be more potent advocates of peace upon earth through the years to come, than this massed multitude of silent witnesses to the desolation of war." Of the 11,954 burials, 8,367 – 70 percent of the total – are unidentified and inscribed with the haunting epitaph "Known unto God." Of the remaining 30 percent, there are two that visitors will want to locate. The grave of Arthur Conway Young, Second Lieutenant with the Royal Irish Fusiliers, carries the simple but potent anti-war message "Sacrificed to the fallacy that war can end war." Canadians will want to find the grave of Private James Peter Robertson, the last of nine Canadian VC recipients during the battle of Passchendaele. Robertson volunteered for the task of silencing a German machine gun that was wreaking havoc on the 27th Battalion. Robertson charged the post, killed four Germans with his bayonet and turned the machine gun around on the remainder of the fleeing soldiers. While carrying the machine gun he led a charge into Passchendaele. Once they had returned to their own lines, they realized two wounded comrades had been left behind. Robertson immediately returned and rescued the first soldier, but was fatally hit by an exploding shell while carrying the second wounded soldier to safety.

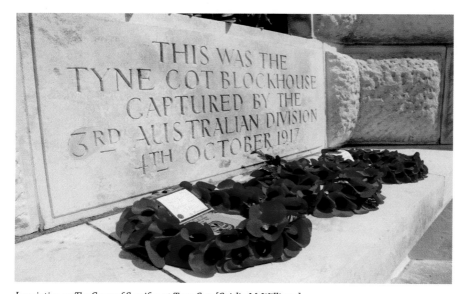

Inscription on The Cross of Sacrifice at Tyne Cot. [Caitlin McWilliams]

Touring the Amiens Battlefields

TOURING AMIENS

TO DO JUSTICE TO the Amiens offensive allocate a day to your tour of the area. You might begin or end the day at the cathedral in Amiens, one of the glories of Western civilization (GPS – 30 Place Notre Dame, Cathédrale, 80000 Amiens, France). Apart from the scale of a Gothic cathedral large enough to hold several Notre Dames, four-hundred carved figures adorn the church with some of the most amazing stained glass windows in France. A number of plaques commemorating regiments and events, especially related to the defence of the city during the German offensive of 1918, hold a prominent place.

If you wish to stay in Amiens there are a number of good hotels and exceptional restaurants. We have stayed in the Best Western L'Univers, an older establishment with comfortable rooms. The Holiday Inn Express and the Carleton are also possibilities but the new Mercure beside the cathedral should be your first choice.

A Begin the battlefield tour at the Australian Memorial near Villers-Bretonneux (GPS – Route de Villers Bretonneux 80800 Fouilloy, France). From Arras take the A1 to the A29 west exiting at Villers-Bretonneaux (Exit 53). Folllow the D23

View from the tower at the Australian National Memorial. [Caitlin McWilliams]

south through the village to the memorial. The cemetery in front of the memorial contains the graves of 266 Canadians including Jean Brillant of the 22nd Battalion. Brillant, who had previously won the Military Cross, won the Victoria Cross during the battle of Amiens. On 8 August 1918, near Méharicourt in France, Brillant singlehandedly neutralized a machine gun position that was holding up the advance of the left flank. Despite being wounded he remained in command and the next day led two platoons against the enemy position when the advance once again stalled. The success of the attack led to the capture of fifteen machine guns and 150 enemy soldiers but Brillant was wounded again. He then led another attack against a German position but this time was critically wounded and collapsed from

The gravestone of Jean Brillant, Victoria Cross recipient. [Nick Lachance]

exhaustion and loss of blood. His VC citation concluded that "Lt. Brillant's wonderful example throughout the day inspired his men with an enthusiasm and dash which largely contributed towards the success of the operation."

There are also 779 Australians buried at Villers-Bretonneux and the memorial lists the names of the 10,700 Australians who have no known grave – a sobering sight. The memorial tower provides an exceptional overview of the Australian sector and the left flank of the Canadian advance. The view is well worth the climb – bring your binoculars.

B There is a small Franco-Australian Museum in Villers-Bretonneux, open daily except Sundays (GPS – 9 Rue Victoria, 80800 Villers-Bretonneux, France). Retrace your steps to Villers-Bretonneux and continue south on the D23. Turn right onto Rue Droit. The museum is located in an old schoolhouse that was originally a gift of Australian school children to the youth of Villers-Bretoneux in honour of the Australian war dead in the area. While much of the commemoration following the First World War featured monuments like Vimy and Thiepval, this schoolhouse bears many similarities to the "progressive" memorials of the Second World War that used the sacrifice to construct something of meaning for future generations like hospitals, parks, and schools. For more information on the museum visit www.museeaustralien.com. You may also wish to visit the striking Australian Monument at le Hamel, the site of the major Australian victory that influenced the plan for the Amiens offensive. The park includes displays and a panoramic view of the battlefield.

C The D23 south from Villers-Bretonneux is the quickest route to the D934 and the Canadian Memorial at Le Quesnel (GPS – D934 80134 Le Quesnel, France) From Villers-Bretonneux turn left on the D934. You will have to make a U-turn once you reach the D41 as the memorial is on the opposite side of the divided highway. The tour map illustrates the routes to the villages that figure in the narrative of the battle but there is little to see except rich farming country, pastoral scenery and pleasant villages. The bridge over the River Luce and the old D934, called Rue du Pont, is barely discernible and it is hard to imagine a 200 metre-wide marsh instead of reclaimed farm land. The villages of Hangard, Démain, and Courcelles were rebuilt after the war. Marcelcave is larger and boasts a (reconstructed) 16th century church of some note as well as a striking Great War monument.

D In a static war where the Cavalry was made redundant by trenches and modern weaponry, the village of Moreuil and the nearby woods were the scene of history's 'Last Great Cavalry Charge' led by the Fort Garry Horse, the Royal Canadian Dragoons and Lord Strathcona's Horse (GPS – D23, 80110 Moreuil, France). Continue toward Amiens on the D934 and take a left heading south on the D23. 1.3 kilometres toward Moreuil you are on the northeast tip of the original battlefield. Farm fields now occupy what used to be the middle section of Moreuil Wood which originally extended to the D23. Pull over before you reach the fork with D28 and the battlefield is on your right. This gives you a commanding view of the battleground from the German perspective. Moreuil Wood was a labyrinth of saplings, heavy undergrowth and Ash trees not yet in bloom in March 1918 which created treacherous conditions for riding. Orders were to delay the German advance as much as possible. The Fort Garry Horse was sent to protect the village. After being driven back on their first attempt, the Royal Canadian Dragoons and elements of Lord Strathcona's Horse dismounted, entered the wood and engaged the enemy in vicious hand to hand combat. Lieutenant Gordon Flowerdew, the Commander of 'C' Squadron discovered two German lines of infantry positions supported by machine guns and ordered the charge. The cavalry passed over both of the lines, killing many Germans. Flowerdew then led his men over the lines again, which caused the enemy to break and run. The cost was heavy with more than 70 percent of 'C' squadron killed or wounded, including Flowerdew who had been shot through both thighs. Those left manned the former enemy positions and held them overnight. It is perhaps ironic that the 'Last Great Cavalry Charge' was made possible by a greater number of dismounted cavalry engaged in close combat. Flowerdew died the next day from his injuries and the Germans soon recaptured and held Moreuil Wood until August.

Canadians interested in the 'Last Great Cavalry Charge' will want to continue

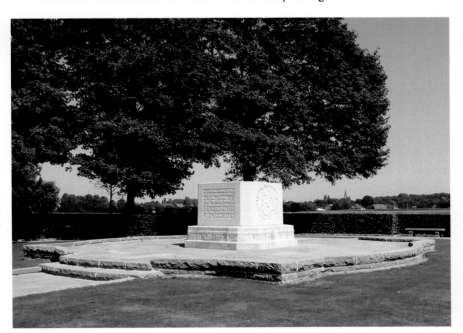

The Canadian Memorial at Le Quesnel. [Eric McGeer]

Sir Alfred Munnings, "Charge of Flowerdew's Squadron." [CWM 19710261-0443]

slightly past Amiens to Namps-au-Val Cemetery where Gordon Flowerdew is buried (GPS – Derrière les Haies 80710 Namps-Maisnil, France). Flowerdew was born in Billingford, Norfolk and emigrated to British Columbia to take up ranching. When war broke out in 1914 he joined Lord Strathcona's horse and rose through the ranks to command 'C' Squadron just before the action at Moreuil Wood. There are several other Commonwealth War Cemeteries in the area and those interested should consult Norm Christie's guidebook The Canadians at Amiens or the Commonwealth War Graves Commission website.

Touring Arras to the Canal du Nord

TOURING ARRAS AND CAMBRAI

A THE START LINE FOR the "Battle of the Scarpe" was located just west of the A1 autoroute. Leaving Arras on the D393 heading to Cambrai you may wish to explore the ground over which Third Division advanced to seize Monchy-le-Preux from the north. Turn left at the traffic circle signed D37 then left again onto the Rue de Feuchy. The road lies close to the start-line of the 8th Canadian Infantry Brigade. It is worth the trip to Orange Hill Cemetery to gain an overview of the position attacked frontally by 5th CMR while 4th CMR worked its way around the main defences before striking south towards Monchy (GPS – Chemin des Revers 62217 Tilloy-lès-Mofflaines, France). Orange Hill Cemetery is one of the smallest Commonwealth cemeteries with 42 Canadian graves and 1 British grave, including a number of Canadian Mounted Rifles (CMR).

B Return toward the D939 and turn left on Boulevard d'Europe and follow the road directly to Monchy-le-Preux. As you enter the village on the Rue de Tilleul look back towards Orange Hill and Arras. In the centre of town, the memorial to the Royal Newfoundland Regiment and the monument to the British 37th

The Newfoundland Memorial at Monchy-Le-Preux. [Matt Symes]

Terry Copp addresses students at the Newfoundland Memorial in Monchy. [Caitlin McWilliams]

Division are of special interest (GPS – 1-5 Rue de la Chaussy 62118 Monchy-le-Preux, France).

Third Division, with Brutinel's Brigade and the Cyclist Battalion on their left flank, advanced to Jigsaw Wood, Boiry-Notre-Dame, and Vis-en-Artois, breaking through the Fresnes-Rouvray Line before handing over control to 4th British Division. To view this optional part of the tour take Rue de Vis southeast to the D34 and turn left toward Boiry-Notre-Dame. Both villages were reduced to ruins before September 1918 and both have been rebuilt largely on their original sites. For those who can read enough French to get by, the Mairie (the Local mayor's office) in Boiry sells two booklets on the history of the village; one on the First World War that includes information on the reconstruction, and one on the occupation in the Second World War (GPS - La Place de Lamotte 62156 Boiry-Notre-Dame, France).

C From Monchy, take the D33 south to D939 east to the Vis-en-Artois British Commonwealth Cemetery (GPS – 1 Route Nationale 62156 Haucourt, France). Among the original 430 graves in Plot I and II there are 297 Canadians. Now, there are 2,342 burials here including 582 Canadians. This is also the site of the Memorial to 9,822 British and South African soldiers who were killed between 8 August 1918 and the Armistice and have no known grave.

To visit the Second Division battlefields, drive west on the D939 to the road signed "Guemappe" (about two kilometres). Turn left on the D34. The village was seized by the 4th Brigade in the initial attack. Continue through Guemappe to a junction and go left to Wancourt in 5th Brigade's sector. The 27th and 28th Battalions had been ordered to turn south to support the British Third Army's stalled advance, capturing Wancourt and pressing forward to the Wancourt Tower located on a low ridge east of the village.

Turn left at the main crossroads in Wancourt, pausing at the British Cemetery which has 246 Canadian burials from 1918 (GPS – 1 Rue d'Alsace 62128 Wancourt, France) – the Cemetery is visible on the right from this point). You are now in the centre of the division's battlefield. The remains of the Wancourt Tower are at the next crossroads. This was the start line for 5th Brigade's attack towards Chérisy.

D Georges Vanier, who later became Canada's Governor-General, lost his leg in this action. Many of his comrades are buried at the Quebec Cemetery which is located in the middle of a farmer's field outside of Chérisy (GPS – D38 62128 Chérisy, France - from here head southeast and take your second left). From the cemetery in Wancourt take Rue d'Alsace south to Chérisy. The cemetery, which is the final resting spot of more than 189 Canadians, is complicated to find. Leave Chérisy on the D38 heading southeast. Take your second left and the cemetery is on your left well into the field. It is worth the walk.

Touring the Canal du Nord and Cambrai

The First Division relieved the Second before the final assault on this section of the Fresnes-Rourray Line began. Though there is nothing to see, the village of Hendencourt-lès-Cagnicourt is within Third Army's sector. To follow this portion of the battle take the D38 south from Chérisy. The division broke through north of Hendecourt, paralleling the advance of 4th Canadian Division astride the Arras-Cambrai road.

E All of this was in preparation for the set-piece attack on the D-Q Line. The D956 from Hendecourt to Dury crosses the line just south of the D939. Return to the Arras-Cambrai road to visit the Canadian Memorial (GPS – D939 62182 Dury, France). The Dury Canadian Memorial, one of the eight sites selected by the Canadian Battlefield Monuments Commission, is on the north side of the highway and is clearly signed with a parking space. The inscription reads:

> The Canadian Corps, 100,000 strong, Attacked at Arras on August 26th 1918. Stormed Successive German Lines and Here on September 2nd Broke and Turned the Main German Position on the Western Front and Reached the Canal Du Nord.

F There are no signs of the trenches or barbed wire that marked the Drocourt-Quéant Line and considerable imagination is needed to relate photographs from 1918 to the pastoral landscape before you. Continue east on the D939 crossing the Canal du Nord, turning right on the D15 to Sains-lès Marquion (GPS – 2 Rue de Baralle 62860 Sains-lès-Marquion, France). As you approach the canal you will see a small parking area and a gravel road leading down to the canal. Park and walk down. The 40th Battalion of the 4th Division won the ground you are standing on. From this vantage point you can see the rising ground west of the canal that provided the Canadians with some protection before the attack.

The Canal du Nord. [Nick Lachance]

While you are near Sains-lès-Marquion you may wish to visit Ontario cemetery which is 1.6 kilometres south of the village on the D15. A large portion of the 257 identified men buried there are from to the Second, Third and Fourth Battalions all raised in Ontario. The original 144 burials are from the fighting for Sains-lès Marquion, the rest were gathered from battlefields and German graveyards after the Armistice (GPS – D15 62860 Sains-lès-Marquion, France).

G Follow the D16 toward Bourlon Wood (GPS – 15-17 Avenue du Bois 62860 Bourlon, France). The route to the Canadian Memorial is well marked at the end of Avenue du Monument. The memorial is located at the top of a stunning set of terraces. The stairs to the memorial are lined with the original shell shattered ancient lime trees that were nursed back to health after the war. Don't miss Bourlon Wood.

Leave Bourlon on the Rue de la Gare returning to the D939 which became the boundary between First and Third Army in the battle for Cambrai. The Canadians as First Army's right flank Corps advanced on the north side of the highway through the Marcoing Line and on towards the Canal de l'Escaut through Sailly-lès-Cambrai, Tilloy and Neuville-Saint-Rémy. Cambrai was finally captured on 9 October when Second Canadian Division crossed the Canal de l'Escaut, seizing the village of Escaudoeuvres and advancing to meet 24th British Division to complete the encirclement. The Third Canadian Division entered the city crossing the canal just north of the D939 or Route d'Arras. The D630 will take you through Neuville-St.Rémy and Escaudoeuvres but there is little to see. (GPS – 18-26 Rue du Pont Rouge 59554 Neuville-Saint-Rémy, France). Cambrai itself was heavily damaged but the central area has been rebuilt.

H Most military tourists will be interested in the well-preserved Mk IV tank "Deborah D51" that was unearthed at Flesquières (www.tank-cambrai.com).

The Canadian Memorial at Bourlon Wood. [Matt Symes]

Canadian soldiers gather in the center of Cambrai. [PA3270]

From Cambrai take the D630 south west and then take a left on the D15 heading south. At Havrincourt veer left on Rue des Calettes and then left again on the D92/ Rue Neuve which takes you directly to Flesquières. Deborah was part of the attack on the Hindenburg Line when it was put out of commission by enemy fire. Four of the eight man crew survived and made it back to their own line, an action that earned Second Lieutenant Frank Heap the Military Cross. When the Allies took control of the ground, the damaged tank was placed into a hole originally dug by the Germans with the intent of building a concrete bunker. The tank was used as a shelter by the British. Contact visite.org@tank-cambrai.com to arrange a visit.

WALKING THE BATTLEFIELDS: BOURLON WOOD

It is possible to start use field lines and boundaries to walk the approximate line of advance for most of the Canadian battalions from the Canal du Nord all the way to the Canadian monument at Bourlon. The wide open fields are much as they were in 1918 and the large distances give some idea of the change in scope from Kitchener's Wood (1915), Desire Trench (1916), and Vimy (1917). However, a walk from the Canal du Nord to Bourlon village is about 4 kilometres which means that

Walking the Battlefields: Bourlon Wood

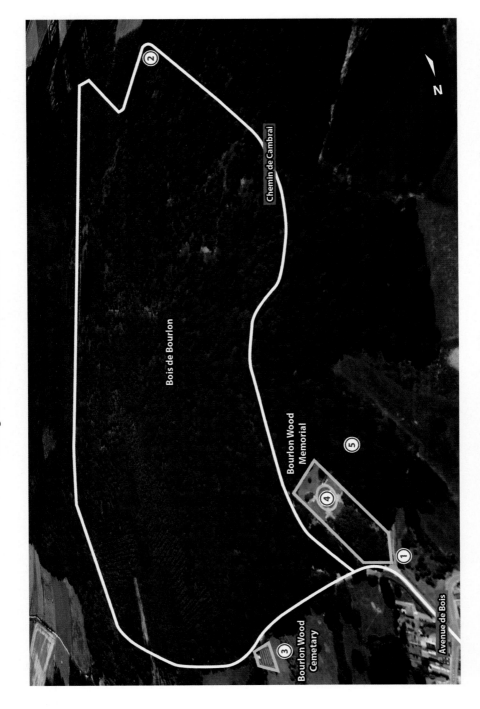

unless you have two vehicles and can be met by one at the other end, it is really not practical.

1/2 We suggest a walk though Bourlon Wood itself. Start at the entrance to the monument down at the road, by the black Canadian National Monument sign. If you feel like a pleasant walk through the woods (about 1.5 kilometres for the full loop), there is a dirt track that leads off around to the east and south of the monument. This trail is often used by local walkers and horseback riders and on its southerly course, follows the approximate course of the German front lines. You will see in the woods remnants of trenches, craters, metal refuse and concrete. Walk towards point 2 and then return or follow the trail around to the north, eventually circling back to Point 3. If it is not a nice day or time is limited, you may choose to venture only a little way into the woods before circling back to the entrance to the monument.

3 From the entrance to the monument, walk to quiet Bourlon Wood Cemetery, about 250 metres to the east-northeast. Follow the track past the memorial to the French resistors executed during the Second World War. Inside the gates you'll find the graves of many of the men who died storming the woods as well as three members of the Chinese Labour Corps. It is a difficult to find, beautiful cemetery and well worth a visit.

4/5 Climb the steps to the monument. If you want to get some idea of the scale of the obstacle taken by the Canadian Corps at the end of September 1918, look back from the top beyond the village below. From this point the Germans were able to observe Canadian preparations and make a concerted defence. Evidence of the fighting is still visible in the woods to the west of the monument. If you push into the brush, you will find deep craters and zig-zag trenches in the forest. These provide evidence of the heavy nature of the fighting encountered by the men buried in Bourlon Wood Cemetery.

Touring Valenciennes to Mons

TOURING VALENCIENNES TO MONS

FOLLOWING THE CANADIANS' ADVANCE to Mons and finishing with a visit to St. Symphorien Cemetery is the classic end of the First World War tour, however the journey is long and only for the devoted battlefield tourist. Mons is less than an hour's drive from Cambrai on the autoroute but in 1918 the advance began on 12 October and ended a month later with the Armistice. If you work your way across country over the Canal de la Sensée through Demain and the Forêt de Raimses, pausing in Valenciennes to plan a set-piece attack from Mont Houy into the heart of the city, some of the difficulties of the last month of the war would become evident.

A To retrace the path of 4th Division in the Battle of Valenciennes, exit the A2 autoroute (Exit 21A) south on the D958 towards Famars. At the roundabout take the third exit onto the D288 and Mont Houy is to your right (GPS – D288 59300 Famars, France). Return to the D958, which becomes Avenue Georges Pompidou. Valenciennes is a busy town of 40,000 which on the whole prefers to forget the years of German occupation and the destruction of parts of the city during the battle.

B Those interested in the conscription crisis will want to visit the St. Roch Cemetery which contains the graves of 151 Canadians including many conscripts (GPS – 103 Avenue Duchesnois 59300 Valenciennes, France).

Return to the A2, which becomes A7, to reach the main square in Mons where the war ended (GPS – Grand'Place 22 7000 Mons, Belgium). Mons is "Bergen" in Flemish, both names remind us of the hill that marks the town. The Grand Place and nearby streets are lined with restaurants in all price ranges. If you are not staying in Mons you might want to avoid trying to park in the city centre.

C The last Allied soldier killed in the war, Canadian Private George Price of the 28th Northwest Battalion, is commemorated by a plaque and a footbridge over the canal which carries his name (GPS – Rue de Mons 2597070 Le Roeulx, Belgium). To get to the walking bridge from the A7, exit onto the B501 and follow it to the R50. Take a left on the R50 continuing around the edge of Mons and take a left onto the N90. From the N90 take a left on the N538/Chassée du Roeulx. Continue on N538 and cross the waterway parallel to the walking bridge on your right. Take your first left toward Ville-Sur-Haine on the N552. Take your first left onto Rue de Mons and the monument is at the foot of the walking bridge at the end of the street.

Price, a 25-year-old from Nova Scotia, was killed by a sniper on 11 November 1918 while searching a house that had been used by German machine gunners. The plaque was originally unveiled on the 50th anniversary of the Armistice by his former comrades on the house where Price died. Widening of the canal led to the destruction of the farmhouse where Price's fellow soldiers tried in vain to keep him alive but the plaque is surrounded by the bricks from the original structure.

D Price's grave, as well as those of the first and last British soldiers killed in the Great War, can be found at St. Symphorien Cemetery (GPS – Rue Nestor Dehon 7030 Mons, Belgium). Retrace your steps back to Mons and when you reach the N90 go east. Follow the N90 east until the roundabout in St. Symphorien and take the first right onto the N564. The well-marked cemetery is about one kilometre down the road. This joint British and German cemetery was constructed by the Germans in 1914. An obelisk erected by the German Army in memory of the German and British soldiers who died near Mons in 1914 dominates the scene. Look for the grave of John Parr, a 16-year-old cyclist scout and the first British casualty of the war. Facing Parr is the grave of George Ellison, the last of almost 900,000 British war dead. In many ways the death of Private George Lawrence Price at 10:58am on 11 November 1918 epitomizes the calamity of the Great War. He was the last soldier killed in a four year conflict that counted almost ten million total war dead including more than 5.5 million Allied casualties. With a population of just over 7.5 million and a mobilized force of more than 620,000, Price was the last of more than 65,000 Canadians and 1,305 Newfoundlanders killed in the "war to end all wars."

TOUR

Mary Riter Hamilton, "Comrades." [LAC 1988-180-122]

THERE COULD BE NO truer measure of the impact of the First World War and its shocking death toll than the efforts made to commemorate the fallen. More than a thousand war cemeteries cluster along the old Western Front, while no fewer than seventeen memorials listing the names of the missing stand in mute testimony to the destructive power of the Great War. One hundred and fifty war cemeteries dot the landscape in the Ypres Salient, two hundred and forty house the dead on the Somme battlefields – each of the battlefield tours will lead you past these "silent cities," and the monuments preserving the memory of Canada's efforts and sacrifice in the Great War. We have therefore included two appendices outlining the Canadian battlefield memorials and the principles which guided the design and construction of the Commonwealth war cemeteries.

OFFICIAL FIRST WORLD WAR CANADIAN MEMORIALS

THE CANADIAN BATTLEFIELDS MEMORIAL Commission (CBMC) was established in 1920. Based on the recommendations of senior officers the Commission selected eight sites (listed below) on which to commemorate the achievements of Canadian soldiers in the Great War. The CBMC launched a national architectural and design competition in December of 1920 and out of the 160 submissions chose seventeen finalists who were then asked to produce a plaster maquette of their design. There was some indecision at first, as it was unclear whether the CBMC wanted eight identical monuments or wished to give certain battles greater significance; but eventually, as Jonathan Vance has noted, "in many ways the outcome of the CBMC's deliberations was governed by the designs submitted...two stood far above the others." What became known as the Brooding Soldier, proposed by Regina sculptor Frederick Clemesha, was selected for St. Julien. What became Canada's most famous war memorial, the twin pylons atop Vimy Ridge, was the creation of Toronto artist Walter Allward. The remaining six locations received identical granite block monuments (each with an inscription commemorating the relevant feat of arms) which were to be placed on a low circular flagstone terrace within a small landscaped park.

CBMC design competition plaster maquettes of finalists in the competition. [VA]

CANADIAN MEMORIALS IN BELGIUM

St. Julien: Commemorating the heroic stand of the First Canadian Division during the gas attack at Ypres in April 1915.

Hill 62: Commemorating the part played by Canadian troops in the defence of Ypres between June and August 1916.

Passchendaele: Commemorating the capture of Crest Farm by the Canadian Corps during the Battle of Passchendaele, October-November 1917.

CANADIAN MEMORIALS IN FRANCE

Courcelette: Commemorating the part played by the Canadian Corps in forcing the Germans back from their defences on the Somme from September to November 1916.

Vimy: Commemorating the capture of Vimy Ridge by the Canadian Corps on 9-12 April 1917.

Le Quesnel: Commemorating the attack by the Canadian Corps, 100,000 strong, on 8 August 1918, which drove the enemy back a distance of eight miles on the first day and commenced the triumphant advance of the Hundred Days.

Dury: Commemorating the capture of the Drocourt-Quéant Switch and the breaking of the Hindenburg Line on 2 September 1918, during the Second Battle of Arras.

Bourlon Wood: Commemorating the crossing of the Canal du Nord, the apture of Bourlon Wood, and the rupture of the final Hindenburg Line defences on 27 September 1918.

NEWFOUNDLAND MEMORIALS IN FRANCE

Beaumont-Hamel: Commemorating the sacrifice made by the Royal Newfoundland Regiment in the Battle of the Somme on 1 July 1916.

Gueudecourt: Commemorating the successful action of the Royal Newfoundland Regiment in the Battle of the Somme on 12 October 1916.

Monchy-le-Preux: Commemorating the Newfoundlanders' participation in the Battle of Arras on 14 April 1917.

Masnières: Commemorating the participation of the Newfoundland Regiment in the Battle of Cambrai on 20 November 1917.

NEWFOUNDLAND MEMORIALS IN BELGIUM

Some of the most striking monuments on the Western Front, featuring the caribou symbol of the Royal Newfoundland Regiment, honour the distinct contribution made by Newfoundland to the Allied cause.

Courtrai (Kortrijk): Commemorating the performance of the Royal Newfoundland Regiment in the Battle of Lys in October 1918.

COMMONWEALTH WAR CEMETERIES

The Imperial War Graves Commission (the Commonwealth War Graves Commission since 1960) was established in 1917. The Commission was responsible for the identification and burial of the war dead of the British Empire, and to maintain the cemeteries and memorials in perpetuity. At the behest of Sir Frederic Kenyon, director of the British Museum, three of the greatest architects of the time, Sir Edwin Lutyens, Sir Herbert Baker, and Sir Reginald Blomfield, worked out the standard design and features for the war cemeteries. One of the most gifted writers in the English language, Rudyard Kipling, was invited to compose the commemorative formulae appropriate to the monuments and headstones. Amidst much deliberation and debate – some of it quite heated, especially on the choice of religious imagery, the use of a headstone as opposed to a cross, and the policy that the dead not be repatriated for private interment but buried among their comrades in the lands where they had fallen – the Commission's guiding principles were laid out in Kenyon's 1918 report:

1. Each of the dead should be commemorated individually by name on a headstone or on a memorial dedicated to the missing.

2. Headstones and memorials should be permanent.

3. Headstones should be uniform in design and the inscription of personal details.

4. There should be no distinction made on account of military or civil rank, race, or creed (although the Commission took great care to observe the traditions of non-Christian or Jewish peoples, such as the Hindus, Sikhs, and Muslims of the Indian Army, or the Chinese who served in labour battalions).

Visitors to the war cemeteries will notice great variety within the uniformity of monumental features. Small battlefield cemeteries may hold as few as forty or fifty burials, where the vast collection cemeteries, such as Etaples or Tyne Cot, contain 11,000 and 12,000 respectively. The cemetery names preserve the names of the old Western Front (Cheddar Villa, Ration Farm, Stump Road) and sometimes the nicknames bestowed by homesick soldiers (Lancashire Cottage, Caesar's Nose, Dud Corner, or the immortal puns on Flemish place names, Bandaghem, Dozinghem, Mendinghem, i.e. "bandage 'em," "dosing 'em," and "mending 'em"). Dominion Cemetery, Toronto Avenue Cemetery, Maple Leaf Cemetery, Quebec Cemetery are a few examples of the names attesting to the Canadians in a given sector.

The cemeteries are usually enclosed by low brick walls and entered through wrought-iron gates, but there is no standard pattern for the interior. In most cases the architects sought to conserve the original outlay wartime burial grounds with their jigsaws of graves huddled around a former dressing station or aid post. Cemeteries with more than forty burials feature Sir Reginald Blomfield's Cross of Sacrifice (with an inlaid Crusader sword), the only overtly religious symbol common to the war cemeteries. Cemeteries with more than a thousand burials will also feature Sir Edwin Lutyens's deliberately neutral Stone of Remembrance, on which the words "Their name liveth for evermore" appear. They were proposed by Rudyard Kipling, who in his regard for the fallen and their families felt that no words of his own could do them justice, and so turned to chapter 44 of the Book of Ecclesiasticus. But as the father of a son listed among the missing, Kipling looked within himself to find the simple, moving formulation "A soldier of the Great War, known unto God," which visitors will see on nearly half of all graves.

Headstones awaiting erection. [CWGC]

Headstone engraving machine. [CWGC]

The headstones over identified burials present the personal details in descending order: regimental insignia (on British graves) or national emblem (a maple leaf, for instance, on Canadian graves); enlistment number and rank; the soldier's name; his unit; date of death and age (if known). A Cross or Star of David was engraved below the register of personal information, but the religious symbol was omitted if the soldier's papers listed no religious affiliation or if his family forbade the inclusion of a religious symbol. For a small cost the families could also have a short valedictory inscription placed beneath the Cross: "Son of my heart, live forever. There is no death for you and me," "The only child of aged parents," "Death is not a barrier to love, Daddy," "The shell that stilled his true young heart broke mine. Mother" – many are indescribably moving and convey the sorrows of the parents, wives, and children, unknown to history, who bore the burden of loss imposed by the Great War for the rest of their lives.

Unlike the sombre French or German cemeteries, the Commonwealth war cemeteries present the aspect of an English cottage garden, in keeping with Kenyon's assertion that "there is no reason why cemeteries should be places of gloom." With this in mind, the architects worked closely with leading horticulturalists to blend flowers and plants native to England with local varieties and to offset the uniformity of white monumental features with the colours of nature. The perfectly

Étaples Military Cemetery. This Commonwealth War Graves Commission cemetery holds over 11,500 dead from both the First and Second World Wars. [Nick Lachance]

manicured lawns and constant maintenance added to the impression of a carefully tended garden that despite its solemnity could become a place of renewal and even hope. In a gesture of reconciliation, German burials were often included in the Commonwealth cemeteries. As the cemeteries took shape during the 1920s and the monuments were raised in honour of the fallen, many felt the sorrow and desire of King Edward VIII as he told a Canadian mother at the unveiling of the Vimy Memorial, "Pray God, madam, it shall not happen again." Sadly and ironically, however, just as the Commission's work was nearing completion in the late 1930s, the Great War resumed in a far more terrible form.

Today more than 900 gardeners tend to the cemeteries of both World Wars. The lawns, plants, and flowers are groomed and replaced when necessary, as are the headstones which the elements have worn or effaced. Five percent of a cemetery is redone each year, so that the whole is redone every twenty years. The bodies of soldiers killed nearly a century ago still emerge from the battlefields, and the Commission makes every effort to identify them, give them an honoured burial, and to contact next of kin. For more information, visit the Commonwealth War Graves Commission website (www.cwgc.org).

ONLINE RESOURCES AND IMAGE CREDITS

THE INTERNET OFFERS MANY opportunities to enrich our understanding of the war and the sites of memory in France and Belgium. Search engines will offer many choices and you will no doubt explore the options on your own, but you might wish to start with www.firstworldwar.com, "a multi-media history of World War One." Almost everything on this site is worth exploring. Click on "Battles" then "Western Front" for excellent, brief descriptions of specific actions. Be sure to listen to the original wartime music in the "Vintage Audio and Video" section. The personal stories in "Memoirs and Diaries," "War in the Air," and "Primary Documents" are all of great interest. Paul Reed's "Battlefields 1918" is an excellent source for photos and maps. www.WW1battlefields.co.uk is aimed at assisting those who tour the actual battlefields. Canadian sites, including Essex Farm, Courcelette, Beaumont-Hamel, are included. The Commonwealth War Graves Commission's website, www.cwgc.org, helps you to locate the graves of individual soldiers. There are brief histories of the main battles and an image browser with photos from the Imperial War Museum. Check the BBC website for World War One. The text offers a revisionist "the war was a remarkable victory" narrative reflecting the views of a group of British historians.

Canadian sites to consult include the audio/visual material at Veterans Affairs Canada (www.veterans.gc.ca/remembers), the Canadian War Museum (www.warmuseum.ca), the Maple Leaf Legacy Project (www.mapleleaflegacy.ca), and King and Empire (www.kingandempire.com) which has an easy to use set of links to other websites. The attestation papers for over 600,000 First World War soldiers, nurses, and chaplains are instantly available online at the Library and Archives Canada (http://www.collectionscanada.gc.ca/databases/cef/index-e.html). The Canadian War Museum offers its own introduction to the First World War including many teacher resources (http://www.warmuseum.ca/cwm/exhibitions/guerre/home-e. aspx). The CBC archives (archives.cbc.ca) is a treasure trove of excellent First World War audio/visual sources including video and radio clips during the war and also the many specials the broadcasting corporation has aired since. As of January of 2009, the National Film Board (www.nfb.ca) has been releasing videos for Canadians to stream online free. If you use the search feature in the top right corner and enter

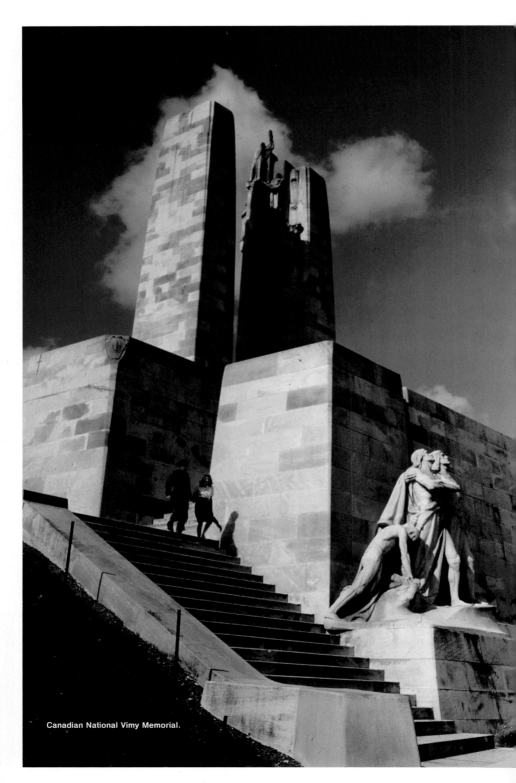

Canadian National Vimy Memorial.

"First World War" you will have a number of documentaries to select from. Last, but not least, check our Centre's website www.canadianmilitaryhistory.ca for links to materials related to this and other guidebooks and publications.

LIST OF WEBSITES AS THEY APPEAR IN THE GUIDE

www.historial.org

www.mapleleaflegacy.ca

www.greatwar. co.uk

www.somme-trench-museum.co.uk

www.somme-battlefields.com.

www.carriere-wellington.com

www.passchendaele.be

www.museeaustralien.com.

www.tank-cambrai.com

www.cwgc.org

www.firstworldwar.com

www.WW1battlefields.co.uk

www.cwgc.org

www.veterans.gc.ca/remembers

www.warmuseum.ca

www.nfb.ca

www.kingandempire.com

www.canadianmilitaryhistory.ca

A NOTE ON PHOTO REFERENCES

CWGC references refer to the Commonwealth War Graves Commission.

CWM references refer to the Canadian War Museum.

GDHI references refer to images from the German Archives.

LAC or PA references refer to images from the Library and Archives Canada.

NAS reference refer to images from The National Archives of Scotland.

PHOTOS WITHOUT CAPTIONS

Page 6: A bayonet, scabbard, and an entrenching tool handle serve as splints on a Canadian soldier whose upper arm has been broken by a piece of shrapnel. [CWM 19930012-696]

Page 97: A student and an instructor use a map to orient themselves atop the Vimy Memorial. [Nick Lachance]

Page 161: A Commonwealth War Graves Commission sculptor at work. [CWGC]